SUSAN GOLD

Toxic Family

TRANSFORMING CHILDHOOD TRAUMA INTO ADULT FREEDOM

TOXIC FAMILY: Transforming Childhood Trauma into Adult Freedom

Published by TVGuestpert Publishing
Copyright © 2023 by Susan Gold

ALL RIGHTS RESERVED. No part of this book may be reproduced or transmitted in any form by any means, electronic or mechanical, including photocopying and recording, or by any information storage and retrieval system, except as may be expressly permitted in writing from the publisher.

ISBN-13: 978-1-7358981-6-2
BISAC CODES: FAM052000, FAM001010, SEL001000

Nationwide Distribution through Ingram
This publication is sold with the understanding that the publisher is not engaged in rendering health care, or other professional services. If professional advice or other expert assistance is required, the services of a competent professional person should be sought. Some names and identifying details have been changed to protect the privacy of individuals.

All brand names and product names used in this book are trademarks, registered trademarks or trade names of their respective holders.

TVGuestpert Publishing is not associated with any product or vendor in this book. TVGuestpert Publishing and the TVG logo are trademarks of TVGuestpert, Inc. TVGuestpert & TVGuestpert Publishing are subsidiaries of TVGuestpert, Inc. TVGuestpert & TVGuestpert Publishing are visionary media companies that seek to educate, enlighten, and entertain the masses with the highest level of integrity. Our full-service production company, publishing house, management, and media development firm promise to engage you creatively and honor you and ourselves, as well as the community, in order to bring about fulfillment and abundance both personally and professionally.

Front Book Cover Design by Tanja Prokop
Book Design by Carole Allen Design Studio
Backcover Author headshot by Mark Savage Photography
About the Author headshot by Tara Shannon

Edited by TVGuestpert Publishing

11664 National Blvd, #345
Los Angeles, CA. 90064
310-584-1504

www.TVGuestpertPublishing.com
www.TVGuestpert.com

First Printing 2023
10 9 8 7 6 5 4 3 2 1

TABLE OF CONTENTS

Acknowledgments vii

Foreword ix

Preface xi

Prelude to Chapter One xiii

CHAPTER ONE: Signing Up for A Rough Journey 1

CHAPTER TWO: Insert Family 5

CHAPTER THREE: Intuiting a Difference 13

CHAPTER FOUR: Bombs, No Shelter 17

CHAPTER FIVE: Burgeoning Betrayal 27

CHAPTER SIX: Fallout from the Family Fray 37

CHAPTER SEVEN: A Path Out of the Jungle 41

CHAPTER EIGHT: Moving Forward 49

CHAPTER NINE: New York, NY 55

CHAPTER TEN: Shifting Geography to Unknown Terrain 65

CHAPTER ELEVEN: The Façade of Love 75

CHAPTER TWELVE: Controlling Fate with Force 87

CHAPTER THIRTEEN: Finding Solid Ground 95

EPILOGUE: 99

A Note From the Author 101

Appendix 103

TOXIC FAMILY

DEDICATION

To little Susie, who never let go and continues to lead me to freedom.

TOXIC FAMILY

ACKNOWLEDGMENTS

Humbly, I acknowledge all of my teachers on this Earth journey in every form. Specific acknowledgments relating directly to this book include Patrick Smith, the first to deliver the message I had a book to write; Jacquie Jordan, New York Times Best-Selling Publisher and forever friend supporting me completely; Belinda Womack and Laura Alden Kamm, reiterating the initial message and not taking no for an answer; Lee Harris, Melanie Tonia Evans, and Alisha Lewis for direct guidance; Sofia Gavura, for serving as inspiration and delivering encouragement; Kamila Smyk-Jaworski, for a very early and affirming read; Nicole Glover, for bravely mushing me through all things involving digital design; and all of my GP friends for opening my heart and delivering the solace of acknowledgment and knowing I'm not alone. Finally, to my family for their roles and love.

TOXIC FAMILY

FOREWORD
THERE'S SOMETHING ABOUT SUSAN

I met her in my late twenties. I knew instantly I wanted to be her friend, but I didn't exactly trust women, especially women in television. My experience had been cutthroat competitive backstabbing women and truthfully, maybe all of that was a reflection of me - yet to be unlearned. Susan was instantly collaborative, compassionate, kind, generous, and funny.

I had never met a woman like her and certainly didn't know a friend like her.

It was an instant girl crush for me with her tight curls, radiant smile, and infectious laugh, coupled with a dose of mystery.

I couldn't figure out what it was about her, but I knew I wanted to be more like her.

It didn't take long, but Susan, without provocation, just with her kindness, became the biggest catalyst of my awakening that would set me off on a, now, twenty-year journey of extraordinary and oftentimes painful discovery of Self.

As you enter the pages of her new book, *Toxic Family: Transforming Childhood Trauma into Adult Freedom*, get ready to be initiated. Living the path of truth and authenticity is not for the weak-hearted, and neither is Susan's truth. Through her journey, you will be activated in your own remembrance and reclamation of the parts of you that need to be healed and transformed all while trusting the loving guidance of your Higher Power through the written coding in her words.

While most books you read are a journey, this will be an activation. You will not be the same person from the beginning of the book as you are at the end of her book. Just like me, I was never the same after meeting her...I only became better.

Jacquie Jordan
TV Producer, NYT Bestselling Publisher, Three-Time Author, and Host of Front & Center with Jacquie Jordan

TOXIC FAMILY

PREFACE

Embracing my humanity to see it as a friend, not something to kick aside, buried in deep shame, or perfect from the outside in is helping me to live with a heavenly perspective here on Earth.

The evolution of my soul through human experience may be the grand prize of this life. Viewing my experiences, even the toughest, as opportunities to triumph in my soul's evolution upon releasing to gain newfound clarity and opening opportunities to practice loving-kindness toward myself and others. I'm able to stand my ground with what I believe in - stand in it, and yet not defend it - which may be the apex of my life's journey.

I want to focus on transforming the brutality of abuse, anxiety, pain, shame, victimhood, and ugliness into triumph, comfort, beauty, and peace. This is what I believe I came here to do.

Susan Gold

PRELUDE TO CHAPTER ONE

The grip of a dark, bumpy, tile floor felt comforting beneath my tiny, angelic-sized feet. At age six, I knew it could all be over if I would plunge the sharp elongated kitchen knife used to carve the grisliest meat into my flat chest.

My pain was visceral as I took the knife from the carving block and surveyed the blade with fascination. Mesmerized, I was wondering what it might feel like if I could find the courage to lance that knife straight through my bleeding heart.

Then I heard her stern tone from the hallway, "Susie, where are you, and WHAT are you doing?" my mom's fierce energy exploded in the kitchen as she came charging through the doorway.

Squatting in front of the open cabinet, I felt no breath while frenetic heat began streaming into my chest, neck, and ears. Quickly, shoving the knife back into its place, I shut the cupboard door.

"WHAT are you doing over there, Susie? Answer me, NOW!" my mom ragefully shrieked as she approached with thunder. I braced myself knowing what I was about to receive.

The hypnotic lure of the knife surrendered, it was time to resume living the hell of a violent, and soul-crushing home life which easily could have been the end of me.

CHAPTER ONE
SIGNING UP FOR A ROUGH JOURNEY

Mystics, astrologers, and channelers say we come to Earth to learn. We sign up for this ride and agree to all details prior to entry. The purpose of life is predestined or planned and key to the evolution of one's soul. I've also been told by multiple intuitive sources it's a high privilege to incarnate on Earth as a human being, especially now during what is described as a golden time of ascension. Masterfully we've earned our role and agreed fully to take on our part, coveting the benefits. Whether true or not, this gives me a strange solace.

The nonsensical and unjust seem clear, the bittersweet more manageable. My present, past, and future join the evolution of my bright and beautiful soul. I've been told my experience is for the betterment of all humankind. This line of thinking keeps me going like a worn, over-trained endurance athlete, rising from the ash repeatedly, standing tall in the exuberance of personal transformation amidst the thick density of planet Earth.

Carrying over from one life to the next, experiences I've had or situations I've encountered repeat in a variety of forms until I embrace and comprehend the lesson I am meant to transform.

Why else would I choose to enter a blisteringly volcanic home, the middle child of a crowded pack (three brothers and a sister) with an alcoholic and narcissistic father and a ragefully depressed, mentally ill mother at the helm? Abuse slathered over every possible area: physical, mental, emotional, sexual, and spiritual. It makes more sense now than when living through it. Perhaps better said, surviving it.

The cauldron and stock of my chaotic upbringing prepared me well to receive more of the same punishment deep into adulthood. I was trained like a brainwashed slave of the Gulag under the bearded patriarchal bluff of somehow remaining safe if I pledged obedience. Deeply entrenched were the beliefs of having to be a good girl to please Mom, Dad, Grandpa, Santa, Jesus, or God only for any scrap of reward to be discriminately swept away, teased just out of reach.

In childhood, I was immersed in anxiety, schooled in neglect, a magnet for use and abuse, and vulnerable prey for a marauder's feast. In adulthood, I placed myself in positions like those I'd experienced as a child, creating them out of some twisted familiarity. When there was no perpetrator or predator in sight, I would masterfully play the role, pitting myself against my own being.

I've spent years delving into those days and hundreds of thousands of dollars on therapy sessions to soothe and assuage them. Some of it is seemingly beneficial, others not. Quite frankly, it's hard to muster the willingness now to live through some of these memories again, enlivening them, and freeing them from their carefully constructed compartments. Ultimately, this is the odd healing balm to discover a treasure chest of deep self-generated love I've unknowingly been seeking, a solid platform from which to launch and land on a cloudless pathway.

It's taken some time to dissect the bloody chords wrapped around my innards from early experiences and initiations leading to invasive trauma still fermenting deep in my soul.

Thankfully, and based on personal experience, I know transformation and healing are possible. I've always had a sense that life truly was meant to be magical, joy-filled, and fun. Intuitively, I knew there was a way of living far different than the life I was exposed to early on and have been living. This knowing has kept me weighted on Earth, ebulliently hopeful of a breakthrough to better humanity.

I feel I was created to be a peacemaker, to bring peace where peace was missing, living partly as an observer, never fully inhaling in my less-than-peaceful family. Often, shrieks echoed: "If you'd get off your f*cking a*s and do something, we'd all be a lot better you selfish b*tch!" accompanied by a deafening pounding on furniture or objects being violently shoved across the room. Separating from my own being, watching my body as if it were a detached instrument playing out traumas below seemed normal to subdue the wounding. Feeling free of anxiety, secure, comfortable, and safe in my own body seemed like a secretly shrouded walkway saved for some special elite.

To my great fortune, my childlike exuberant belief in magic and joy was never completely trained or drained out of me. It was one boundary I would protect with all I had to put forth for my own survival. I knew this instinctually.

I didn't know how to find smoother roads and had few practical tools for navigation. The Universe and the Divine would step in with miracles whisking me away to better terrain and delivering angelic gauze to heal the wounding.

I spent years wrapped defensively in pretend layers of carefully packed emotionless plastic, a Knight's armor earned early on the battlefield of my family home. Self-induced, this faulty protective wrapping seemed to keep me safe, a distance apart from others. I could play the role of engaging well, smiling, and pleasing. It was fraudulent. I was hoping I could melt those layers built like a maudlin fortress around me and break free from my isolation. It would be a lot of living through mistakes and miracles to heal gaping encrusted wounds branded prematurely to see it all in a different light.

The abuse of my childhood was magnified by the abuse my parents had experienced. And their abuse was magnified again by the abuse their parents suffered. Damaged children abusing damaged and abused children and surrendering blame there. Discovering this has helped me find forgiveness and come to know compassion for my perpetrators, myself, and for humankind.

The rough journey issued holds merit and has been key to an inner flowering for which I'm grateful. To feel peace, contentment, my feet on the ground, richness in my breath, and genuine warmth in my heart toward myself and others is a miraculous refuge compared with an eternally hypervigilant engine of a discordant central nervous system. To find beauty in simple moments, and a deep inner peace otherwise inaccessible, are gifts of a lifetime. They are the non-material brocades embracing me now. Hard fought for yet won after escaping a virtual maze that had me in some unyielding state of eternal and damning hypnosis.

While the experiences I've traversed are important to the story, what I'm more intrigued with is how I choose to transform each one, rising with love. Releasing the forgetfulness of who I am at the core of my soul and waking up out of a deep state of amnesia may be my unparalleled triumph.

There are episodes and experiences I view as shameful, damning, or dishonorable which I would rather ignore. What I've come to realize is that these are the exact experiences key for me to review, embrace, and consider from a higher perspective, one of heaven.

Experiencing a life review here and now, while I'm still on Earth, is leading me to a less dense, fear-reduced existence. Accessing my deeply wounded child self, recognizing her innocence, and reclaiming her energy and power, renewed and restored, are delivering inner compassion, a profound elixir.

TOXIC FAMILY

CHAPTER TWO
INSERT FAMILY

My father was one of two boys born to a nothing's-good-enough tyrant of a father and a mother who put her eldest son, my dad, up on a pedestal of doing no wrong to try and compensate. He was dutiful and toed the line going to college and pursuing advanced degrees to secure a safe job far away from subjects he loved - history and music.

Drinking alcohol helped my father cover his buried emotions and desires as well as transform harsh memories into wild adventures. Romanticizing his childhood and upbringing allowed him to submerge his inner wounds. Plying himself with alcohol shellacked those memories into place.

Not really having space or desire to get to know his own worth or value and feeling a sense of responsibility, he ended up marrying my mother after a very brief courtship. "Oh well, I oughta do this," was how he described making the decision when I asked during a car trip we made together.

My parents were set up on a blind date for a fraternity dance. She came from Ohio; he was in Pennsylvania. She was fun, talented, intelligent, and outgoing. He was handsome and charming, in a boyish way, heading for academic excellence. The plan was she would work to help put him through school for a master's degree and a Ph.D., and then it would be her turn.

Her turn never came.

What did come were five children in very short succession, and plenty of martyrdom. We were all considered accidents brought on by Catholicism – even with temperature checking with a thermometer to decipher fertile periods of ovulation for abstinence. A philandering husband was the cherry on top of the five-pack parcel. Emotions of rage, anger, and a non-transferrable feeling of being stuck cemented my mother's torment of living a matriarchal nightmare.

From my father's own experience, growing up with a doting mother, he only knew women were to serve and maybe more precisely stated, serve him. He remained a boy trapped in a man's body and really didn't have much concern for those he used and abused by his behavior along the way. When he'd recover from an alcoholic blur long enough to regain some semblance of consciousness there would be nothing but a bucket of shame to hide and drown once more in the drink.

Devout, my mom had three children, including me, before she was twenty-six and another two before she was thirty. With each of her five 'accidental' births came mounds of postpartum depression and the realization she had married someone who had no desire, whatsoever, to show up as an adult. He couldn't. The seed of narcissism was planted.

The last time my mom agreed to visit her in-laws, who lived in a small New Jersey town across the bridge from Philadelphia, she was pregnant with child number four. My brother, sister, and I energetically bounced out of the car after a long drive ready to cause chaos when my PopPop flew into a rage screaming in front of all of us and directly at my mother, "Why did you have to have so many damn kids!" She tried vainly to physically shield my brother, sister, and me from PopPop's words huddling us together. In my grandfather's eyes, having children was solely her fault.

My mother tried to be the perfect wife, ignoring my father's wandering eye and the full-on cheating that began almost during the honeymoon. Her buttons were not just pushed, they were smashed. Compulsively, she'd twist her hair around her index finger, almost pulling it from her skull, anxious and ready to explode. Somatic sensations of her severe abuse as a child would erupt. She tried with all her might to repress horrific memories by ladling on pound after pound of excess flesh to fortify herself, seeking safety, and an exit from deep misery.

My mother was one of two children born post-World War II. When informed his firstborn was not a boy, her own father did not go to the hospital to see his wife and newborn baby girl. My mom never escaped feeling she was a bastard child and wore it on her sleeve bouncing between the victim and righteously misaligned.

My maternal grandmother was forbidden to show affection toward her children. My grandfather's own beloved mother died when he was young leaving

CHAPTER TWO   Insert Family

him with an extremely abusive and punishing stepmother. By repressing his own wife's desire to shower their children with love, he thought he was doing them a service. My grandfather had been beaten, almost to the point of death, by his stepmother which contributed to his own struggle with mental illness and would later bring on psychotic episodes.

My grandfather would physically project onto my mother the very abuse he had suffered as a child. It would come out of the blue and in dangerous heaps. When it was done, my mother was forbidden to talk about it. She was silenced and expected to keep up appearances, acting as if everything was fine, a seemingly perfect front more important than anything else, including her own psyche.

My mother's mother resigned herself to martyrdom and denial as well as serious diabetes, complete with gangrene holes in the soles of her feet. My mother followed the pattern of her mother's emotional state which turned out to be a dangerous and brutal cocktail from which she could never escape. This contributed to creating an illness similar to her father's, one that was mental.

My mother's split between solid reality and her true self began early in her childhood. It was compounded when she was molested by the Parish priest. She didn't have a chance. She hid her imbalance the best she could. Trauma ran deep and transformed into a bottomless pit of low self-worth and an unending vat of deep personal shame. She worked to hide it by excelling in school, in sports, and in domestic achievement, yet there was only so much anger she could compress.

Her childhood experience created a bonfire of rage erupting from her core like a volcano. Usually signaled by a brutal slur of cursing, "Jezus Fu*k#ng Chr**t, get up here (insert name of a child, dog, husband) before I kill you!" she'd yowl like a beleaguered wild and rabid cat.

By the time I came on the scene even my mother's womb was not safe. Her hatred and confusion penetrated the placenta. Her deep postpartum depression exacerbated her mental illness now with another child to contend with, a darkly impish husband who looked like the hero, absolute scorn from her in-laws, and judgment from her own parents.

With an absent, philandering, drunken Peter Pan as a spouse and three children under the age of four to contend with, she was saddled and confined to relentless drudgery. Mass quantities of laundry, making meals on a nickel, and constantly cleaning up ravaged rooms, equaled mountains of overwhelm. Inexplicable oncoming betrayals from her partner were her reward. Magnificently, she replayed the horrors of her own childhood with her own self-created family.

My father clearly did not realize what he'd gotten into, and he certainly didn't sign up for what he perceived as his wife's brutality. There was continual drama and not enough of anything to go around. Certainly not a drop of wholesome undiluted love.

My mom loved homemaking. She was highly gifted and very smart, maybe smarter than my astrophysicist father. I remember her at the ironing board when I came home from school, working on a dress or pair of my father's slacks, preparing a homemade meal for us, and finishing a birthday cake she'd made from scratch.

And then there was her other side…screaming voraciously, throwing things, crying into her clenched and gnarled fist. I have a vague memory of being under two years of age, in my playpen for much longer than I could tolerate. Grabbing the wood slats, feeling the small plastic padding adding a bounce under my feet wailing for my "mamma" as my face went red, and wet with tears. Rather than an urge to comfort, this drew a surge of rapacious wrath from my mother. My cries were met with physical force, coupled with a brutal sense of rejection, abandonment, and confusion.

Her moods were like a violent unscheduled roller coaster. You never knew what you could get around the next turn. "Come sit with me Susie," she'd say, giving me a loving cuddle. Moments later she'd be throwing an object across the room at my oldest brother seething while I remained beside her, frozen and breathless. Her paranoia was explosive, and her temperament could change on a dime. It was best to attempt to find cover, hope for invisibility, and pray your name wouldn't be called.

What I latched onto was the sadness oozing from her pores. I wanted to fix it with all my might. I witnessed her utter self-hatred, a deep sense of being ill at ease and continually on edge. She'd be listening to some voice somewhere else, her eyes fixed off into the distance, twirling her hair with pressure between her index finger and thumb while sipping stale black coffee from a ceramic mug, and laughing shrilly.

Most confusing was her power to love was as great as her hate and rage. Her creativity and energy were almost unmatched. One Halloween she made a train out of cardboard boxes, each of us playing the role of a different car. I was proud of her and excited to come home from school that day and try on my assigned car. It was a last-minute project and she worked frantically even as we began to march down Market Street toward the judge's stand.

"Bobby," she yelled at my oldest brother, black dust smudged on his face. He'd been pretending to shovel coal into the engine leading in the locomotive, complete with steam coming out of a tall spout rigged with dry ice, "slow down in front of the judging stand!" she frantically ordered.

There was total elation when my mom learned we had won first prize with a picture to verify it splashed across the front page of our local newspaper. She was completely capable of creating magic. It was almost always with deep panic and by the seat of her pants, yet she embraced the drama and relished

CHAPTER TWO Insert Family

each victory.

One summer, she coached the springboard diving team of the youth league in our town. She was obese, yet she had so much grace in taking off of the platform backward. She loved showing us how to step, step, lift, hop and jump from the deck. Our diving team placed well. I came home relishing a blue, first-place ribbon.

Our home was usually decorated for each Holiday including the smaller ones like St. Patrick's Day or Labor Day and there were festive foods and gatherings. I wanted to believe our family was intact, friendly, and safe like those of a Currier and Ives Christmas card but that was far from the truth.

At around four years old, I had a terrifying experience with my mother that left me with a long-lasting negative effect. We were in the small bathroom upstairs, ceiling pitched making a tight triangle, which all seven of us shared. My mom was bathing us one by one. There were striped faded towels on the floor and a clawfoot bathtub with gray water half full after multiple bathers. It was my turn to get in. Excited for my moment, I stepped up.

My mommy went rigid for a moment and then snapped, her eyes becoming snakelike slits, "You little brat," she screamed out of nowhere, "why are you so bad!"

Barely breathing while trying to hide in full view, I was wishing my nice mommy would come back. Desperately, I was grasping for what I had done to make my mommy so mad in an instant. Completely vulnerable, I was like the baby bird I collected earlier that had fallen from its nest, trying to stifle sobs of fear replacing what moments before had been a joy.

She dug her hands into my flesh, pulling me close, her fingernails penetrating, starting in a loud whisper with a crescendo into a full scream, "You nasty spoiled, selfish girl!" raising her forearm and hitting me hard. I fell back stunned, bringing on even more tears.

"You want to cry? I'll give you something to cry about!" she shrieked her palm open, fingers forcibly together slapping me again and again. The room got hot, began to swirl, and then turned brown. I struggled to bring myself back into my body, into the bathroom thinking my mommy was a monster I wasn't sure I could survive. Under fathomless fear and hurt was an insatiable desire to help my mommy feel better so this wouldn't happen again.

Seemingly indelible markings splattered through my belief system. When I see young children around four years old, it stuns me to imagine the untethered and brutal force I was surviving. My mother's erratic behavior was shattering my willowy frame. My small brain was incapable of processing it. I couldn't understand why my mommy was sometimes so nice and other times so mean. I didn't understand why I was so bad at causing untethered changes in her temperament. I only wanted to fix it. Desperately.

I knew to my little bones I was unsafe. For no reason, and at any moment, things could shift and become dangerous. Obediently, I was taking on the blame for being the reason for her trauma. Co-dependency began early and ran deep. The pattern of wanting to take care of and become responsible for the chaotic behavior of others was ingrained very early as a survival tool. My breathing changed, overall. It was now often shallow. I learned to become hypervigilant, monitoring everything. Anxiety began to build along with a desire to make myself invisible.

My mom's unsteadiness was coupled with my dad playing the role of absolute champion whenever he'd finally walk through the front door. He seemed like a savior and hero.

He'd grab me from the ground and lift me up high over his head to ask, "Are you a tiger or a baby?" to which I'd dutifully respond, "A TIGER!" Quickly, I'd shut down any complaint I wanted to make.

There was an odd smell to my dad. It was whiskey mixed with SCOPE and Old Spice seeping from his skin. He loved to dole out whisker hugs with a red-faced smelly smile that burned my little cheeks.

As I matured, I realized this early training, to be on guard, deny my feelings and present a stoic front, gave me license to show solidarity with whoever gave me attention, shutting down tight to any sense of self-nurturing or self-care as I matured. I was going to be a TIGER.

There was little room to show vulnerability, no space for indulgence, and only a modicum of kindness as one in a family of seven with two unstable pseudo-adults at the helm. We were being brought up to have few needs, to be fiercely independent, and to have little regard for our own safety or well-being. It was a badge of honor.

By the time I was five, the explosive rage toward me grew along with the violence between my parents. I woke up one morning to find my father next to my mother in bed wearing a full arm cast. The window was broken, and freezing air was coming through the punctured hole. My dad told me with a laugh: "I got mad at your mother and punched my arm through the window in the middle of the night. It was dumb." I couldn't take in the full circumstance. I was shocked by the scene and the odd feeling in the room. There was something sinister lingering as I stared at the light white sheer curtains blowing with bitterly cold air flowing through the opening.

While my father was making light of what happened, I felt frightened. I didn't feel safe. Something was very wrong, and I could actively sense the thickness of it. I was finely attuned to energy but didn't know it. My mom seemed disconnected; she was gritting her molars, cheeks taught, speechless, and sullen. She was looking away toward the side of the room. Denial of the truth, efforts to make light of darkness and monstrous veils over healthy communication were my takeaway.

CHAPTER TWO Insert Family

I wanted more than anything to make the ominous feeling in the bedroom disappear. I was searching for a way to make it better and glue my mommy and daddy back together again, a behavior that would echo and repeat for years between myself, abusive partners, relationships, and situations in the workplace. Ultimately, I felt helpless and afraid of what might come, my sleepy dreams and projections becoming more regular nightmares.

I was learning not to trust. The world was unpredictable. People who said they loved you could hurt you and love could smell like liquor and feel like lies and drama. Family equaled drama. Marriage equaled obedience. Love equaled danger. Dry combustible tension in the air, knowing everything could explode without notice was not only a way of life but of love. It was the perfect basic combat boot training for what would become part of my own pain-ensnared future.

Trying to appease it, to be a perfectly good girl in an attempt to freeze a murky river of violence and receive the attention and care I craved became a dysfunctional tool of choice. Fantasy helped me release the anxiety beginning to snowball. I created magical 'friends' who would come to visit and approve of me. The energy of angels would rescue me. Eating as much sugar as I could access softened blows of intense anxiety, feeling unloved, and alone with no safe recourse.

Sunday afternoons were sometimes spent wandering through the woods, surrounded by nature as a family. Being among ferns, miniature pinecones, moss, tall pine trees and the whispering wind was soothing yet tainted. I was usually on guard waiting for spontaneous anger to erupt.

Sunday evenings were generally a time of feeling special and safe in front of the TV on the floor, all five of us squeaky clean in our footie pajamas, a few toes poking out of holes, watching Tinkerbell set off fireworks above Disney Castle. There were cartoons and an episode of *Old Yeller* or *Winnie the Pooh* with my dad serving us root beer floats. Vanilla artificially flavored ice cream, store-brand root beer, an extra-long spoon, and a straw in a plastic pastel-colored cup, often with teeth marks around the rim, brought happiness.

My baby blanket soothed me. It was worn, the satin border separating from the quilting, threads peeling, never quite coming clean after a wash and dry. I took my tattered treasure everywhere. My blanket was my friend, a constant, reliable companion, and a soft sense of knowing all would be alright, somehow.

At five, I took my beloved blanket on one of our semi-annual trips in our white Pontiac Catalina station wagon to visit my mom's parents, Grammy and Grandpa, in Ohio. I was excited to get there. During our stay, I couldn't find my blanket and panicked. My mother came looking for me and asked me to go down into the basement with her. My grandfather, her father, was standing on the barren, immaculate, crack-less concrete floor next to the incinerator.

I slowed my step, wondering what was happening. My grandpa urged me closer. "Step up on this stool," he said, opening the incinerator lid.

Reluctantly, I obeyed. Peering over the edge of the incinerator were the still smoldering silken remains of my treasured confidant, glistening orange, and black in a pulsating blob of ash.

I felt a lump forming in my throat. Stunned and angry I knew I couldn't cry. I'd be punished, hit, or mocked. I bit my bottom lip hard, the lump in the back of my throat expanding as I was swallowing tears.

My grandpa, who I loved, had a shaming stern tone, "You're a big girl now, and you don't need that dirty blanket anymore!" He smiled. My mother while supporting him, standing by in silence, slowly lifted her shoulders toward her earlobes. I felt obliterated. I couldn't believe they would both co-mingle and conspire this way. Violation soaking deeply into my pores, something inside me went deadeningly dim.

The shock was ferocious. My trust in my mother and my grandfather was shattered. Wordless and numb, I turned on my heel, silently climbing the stairs to find a safe corner releasing all my trapped tears on my own, asking no one to help soothe my pain. I already knew I couldn't trust.

Here was another traumatic memory to bury deep into the corners of my being finding its own way to rot.

My childlike belief in people with power who were to be loving eroded, and I began building a shell around my insides trying to find what felt like protection from damage continuing like the drip of a faucet. My shell hardened.

Shutting down was the only way I knew to contend with what I faced. There was no blanket to physically project my fears, anxiety, and pain. I began to use my own body, savagely chewing on my nails and cuticles, and binging on sugar.

Now an ability to see the truth seemed to be slipping away, something I'd rather repress. Intuitively, I knew it was important to maintain light and vision, but it was becoming too painful to try. Standing out in this area seemed only to serve in bringing me harsh gut-wrenching lessons. I felt I didn't belong in my own family and maybe even beyond. Though I was very young, I remember trying to speak the truth and hold on to the truth. Now I was weary, sensing I was alone, and on my own, way before my time.

CHAPTER THREE
INTUITING A DIFFERENCE

Though I liked school, it multiplied the anxiety I was feeling. I aimed hard to please and was a good student. I didn't feel I fell automatically in line like everyone else, robotically towing the suggested line. I had a strong will and was stubborn. I also had a sense of inner knowing that seemed different from other children and teachers. I wondered if there was some mistake, I didn't belong.

In Kindergarten, my teacher invited me to a special table with Rose Hunter, a blonde-haired, blue-eyed girl with thick Coke glass, and pink-rimmed eyewear. At first, I was excited to be singled out. Was I being recognized as special? There was a man in a suit waiting for us and with the teacher's approval, he asked us to begin to practice writing our names on the piece of off-white paper with thin, blue ruled lines in front of us using our right hand, instead of our left. Suspicion and anger welled up in me. Rose dutifully obeyed.

Coaxing me in a whisper, the man said, "Please take this pencil, put it in your right hand, and spell your name."

I didn't say anything, looked away, and began to pout. I could feel my whole body pull inward. My Kindergarten teacher looked over, annoyed. I felt burning in my chest and neck from resisting when I caught a still voice inside of me calmly reaffirming my decision. Eventually, I wore my teacher down and the man in the suit down. There was no more talk of me switching hands for writing.

This inner strength and knowing were natural. I sensed early on it had to stay intact. It was a very clear voice of knowing. If I listened, it would guide me gently. It came from inside and seemed like an authentic friend I could access at will and rely upon in all circumstances. I could trust that voice completely.

My days were lonely, even amongst three brothers and a sister. Out in the yard, I'd look up to the sky and wish myself onto clouds to seek solace and safety. I'd whisper to angels I assumed were hovering in the air, "Can you help me get up to you and escape?" I sensed angels were at the church we attended every Sunday that was up the block from our house. Usually, I'd plead to them, "Help me, I'm scared, please help me."

I'd watch the birds unrestrained and soaring and would wonder about my life here on earth. I sensed I was here for a reason yet felt trapped. What had I done so wrong to be experiencing all I was, and why did I feel so unsafe? Why was my home life so unpredictable and fear so deep?

I had no idea that some of the feelings I was carrying did not all belong to me. They were projected by my family, society, and the collective density of living a human life on Earth. I was very young, struggling to keep my head above water while holding my own beliefs that life was supposed to be joyful, and that I deserved to feel safe, secure, and loved. I was drowning in negativity, fear, and abuse and had to figure out how to continue to stay afloat.

In Sunday school, I got a heart-cracking message from a short and somewhat broad, Sister Consuela, nicknamed "Sister Pussywillow." This nun was stern and had a reputation for conveying blame. She seemed on a mission to convince me I was a bad and sinful girl. A very bad, and sinful girl. I remember sitting on a cold aluminum folding chair, my eyes glued to the cement floor covered in tan and white linoleum squares with gray flecks, feeling the burn in my gut of guilt over my 'badness.' Sister would clench her fist over her heart and press her crucifix on a chain into her bosom, "You have caused Jesus to die on the cross, God will never forgive you for that sin, EVER. His only son suffered and died for you," she stabbed her index finger pointing toward me like a deadly laser.

The thought I killed Jesus ripped into my vulnerable and open heart. The very idea was riveting in a horrific way. I was filled with shock and self-disgust trying to digest this seeming truth. And every Sunday, in a literal form, I faced God's only son, as a bloody statue hanging high, center stage on the altar confirming my absolute abomination.

It would be five decades before I would realize I was still internalizing the belief Sister Consuela fostered. God hated me for killing his only son, I deserved punishment and persecution for my grave transgression. Nothing I could do would ever make up for this offense except hang myself on a cross after being trained with this imprisoning belief.

When I'd get free of self-condemnation, I could usually access a feeling in my body that there was more, and what I was living wasn't the only truth. Maybe it wasn't the truth at all. I somehow sensed I was destined for brighter living and that it would come one day. I just had to hold on and have faith.

Our family moved to a large house across the street. It seemed like a mansion compared with the small brick half of a house the college had leased us. Little did I know that in it, I would have profound initiations. It would be a treacherous road away to come to interpret these experiences as positive initiations.

CHAPTER THREE Intuiting a Difference

There was magic in having more bedrooms, French doors to open in the living room and a balcony upstairs off another sole bathroom for seven. Friends of my moms came to help us scrub and somehow, we made the transition.

I walked to and from school most days on my own. Our family was right on the borderline of the school bus service. I didn't mind walking. My mom would often drive us to school on rainy days or in the snowy months, a coat thrown haphazardly over her nightgown, and fake fur slippers traipsing through inches of precipitation. Coming out of school at the end of the day, I often wished my mom would be waiting, car idling, warm, and comfortable. I'd watch with envy at the other kids who had rides or parents waiting to walk with them down the block and at home. If I happened to be walking out with my friend Kristen Minnick, sometimes she'd ask her mom to give me a ride in their red and white Rambler station wagon.

"Come on in, Susie," her mom would smile leaning toward the window, unlocking the doors while lighting her cigarette with the car lighter. My heart would leap with joy. We'd hop in, smoke twirling from the front seat seeping toward the back.

Mrs. Groce, newly married, was my first-grade teacher. I fantasized about what her wedding might have been like and what her new life might be like now with her husband. I imagined them very much in love and content. She was tall and very thin, and her last name was the same as mine, we just spelled them differently. She didn't seem uncomfortable at all to have a last name that was similar to a term of disgust. I was happy to study her perfectly styled hair, thanks to what must have been at least half a bottle of Halo hairspray. It was mesmerizing to watch her gold bracelet with the safety chain clang around her boney wrist. She seemed sophisticated, elegant, and seemed happy. Her green eyes and peach lipstick beamed. I wondered if my mom could ever be that way. I wanted my mom to be thin, coiffed and beaming. I wanted her to be loved by my dad and glow like my teacher, the newlywed. Mrs. Groce didn't have children. She could leave her first-grade students behind at the end of the day in the classroom. My mom couldn't. She was stuck with all five of us. All the time. And she let us know it often.

One slushy cold classroom day we all got a mimeographed sheet with the face of Abe Lincoln to color in honor of his birthday. After smelling the damp, fresh scent of the drying ink, I decided to use an orange crayon to color Honorable Abe's face rather than the brown crayon suggested by Mrs. Groce. It made no sense to me to use brown, orange seemed more natural.

Jeff, my classmate at the desk to my left, raised his hand while staring at my coloring sheet, tattling on my 'rule-breaking.' Mrs. Groce came over to my desk to look.

I felt familiar red-hot shame rising, "Next time, follow directions, Susie," she said in a creamy tone of admonishment. My heart sank to my toes.

I didn't really understand this school stuff. Attempts at forcing me to write with another hand, and now coloring Abe Lincoln's face only a certain color didn't add up. Where was the joy of exploration? It seemed I was to convert to a standard format and become obedient. I had little interest in that premise. It didn't seem right to me that we were here on Earth to be obedient.

Underneath my shame and desire to fit in, there was a burning to be authentic and not what a standardized template wanted from me. Intuitively, I imagined a place where people wouldn't question my reasoning or judgment, and creativity would be welcomed. I had to make the best of it in my little town until I could get to that "other" place.

A kernel of solid belief in myself kept that little flame of light burning inside of me. An inner knowing to see beyond what was presented seemed pivotal. If I'd fall in line, asleep, I'd lose myself. Knowing this added to a burgeoning pool of anxiety and fear.

Sugar remained my solace and consistent comfort, along with my family pets. After another visit to see our grandparents in Ohio, they packed bags full of treats for the long car ride home. I was way back in the rear of the station wagon close to the bags and started rifling through them. Crème-filled Oreos were the magic ticket to escape. I quietly ripped into the plastic covering, being sure I wasn't heard or seen. Reaching inside the package, I freed my first cookie. Relief came instantly followed by the fear of being caught. I reached back in for another, and another. With each cookie I ate, I felt a sneaky and imperious urge for the next one. My stomach tightened, then began to twist, after eating a row of cookies. There was no stopping me. I was hardly chewing. Maybe three chews and the next cookie was in my mouth. I began to almost smash the cookies into my mouth. My head began to ache and swirl. Three hours into an eight-hour trip, I had Oreos coming out of my nose trying to find safety and escape whatever feelings of insecurity, and judgment had been dished out directly or expressed subconsciously during our stay.

I didn't know it to be odd then, but I could read the energy of others quite clearly. I knew more about watching the subtle silent movements and gestures than what was being officially presented. I could grasp an inner dialogue that was meant to be private as if it were being expressed publicly. It was something I could turn on and turn off. Generally, I was left holding a bag of unprocessed emotions and secrets that didn't belong to me.

Overeating, undereating, secret binging, and purging with movement kept me on a maudlin tilt-a-whirl of secrecy and self-hate to try and obliterate the emotions I tried to avoid feeling. I had to hide what was my sensitivity and intuition, it wasn't safe. I didn't know quite how to cope and there was no one to confide in that I could trust and count on completely. My pets, trees, angels, and seemingly sugar were my comfort.

CHAPTER FOUR
BOMBS, NO SHELTER

A feeling of impending doom, edgy discomfort and constant need for defensiveness was becoming my 'normal' triangular range of emotion. Rather than blood, I'm sure more anxiety coursed through my veins. Quaking under my feet, no solid ground to trust, and no dependable platform of support became familiar. I felt a wide-open, free flow of abuse coupled with a landslide of shame and guilt injected into the cells of my being. It was my daily bread. My family members, classmates, priests, nuns, teachers, and friends in my small town seemed schooled in the same frequency. With the trauma, my childhood was tossed into the sewer.

Ingrained by institutions, society, and my family, there was not enough for all, and fierce competition was necessary to survive, it was me against you. While professing charity and kindness, I learned you were to secretly covet what was yours and protect it at all costs. If you didn't do good to others, you could go to church on Saturday night or Sunday morning to make up for it all and start again from zero.

Often, I felt like Cinderella minus the Grand Ball and Prince. Each day after school, I'd come home to a long list of chores outlined in a scrap paper note from my mother. Written by hand in cursive with blue pen, occasionally a little secretarial shorthand creeping into the list, I was expected to complete the saga of duties before I touched homework or went off to dance class. Over time, I would see those notes and want to tear them to shreds, the rage squeezing my chest, my body burning with an angry heat of seeming injustice. I wouldn't dare speak up or revolt as that would bring on physical punishment. Instead, I used a steely focus to get everything done, quickly multitasking when possible.

My portion of the note would usually include orders like vacuuming the downstairs rooms dusting the living room – including the corners and baseboards; taking the laundry from upstairs down into the basement; carrying all the things on the stairs to go up, upstairs; making sure the laundry on my bed was folded. It seemed like a long list for a second grader and unfair compared to the note for my three brothers which often read: "take out the trash" or "feed the dog."

Later I'd see how the notes helped me to become incredibly organized, laser-focused, and able to execute large tasks efficiently minus help. The burden of being overly responsible so young became a chafing yoke deep into adulthood.

My mom seemed like a tyrant and bully with never-ending requests to serve, mostly her. Sometimes, I'd just be done with the list when the white wall phone would ring. Reluctantly, I'd answer, and it would be my mother, "Susie, I forgot to ask, please go sweep the front porch before you leave the house and pick up any toys out in the side yard, I don't want to see anything out there when I get home."

When a chore was not done to my mom's measure of excellence, I was lambasted. Even if I tried to please her purposefully to help her feel a little bit better, somehow, I couldn't meet the mark. Instead, I'd be on the receiving end of criticism or rageful punishment. It was hard to believe my mom was that angry, no, make that rageful. It oozed from her pores, the explosions unpredictable. I wanted to wave a wand and make her violence disappear for her happiness as well as for my own safety and that of my younger siblings.

On the other extreme, my dad was the emblem of excitement and fun. After a lot of spelunking later in life, I'd see through his disguise. Excelling at academics, athletics, and adventures in the great outdoors was a way to try and attract his undivided attention, and acceptance. It didn't matter how little you were, how cold, frightened, or traumatized, he'd be taking jabs and jeers to spurn you forward with little regard for your safety and comfort. "Susie, keep up! You can't lag or we'll leave you and you'll be lost!" he'd threaten with a sarcastic laugh. I was reluctant not to step up and try to fulfill his challenging commands ignoring my own needs. I was desperate for recognition, especially his.

I remember my dad teaching me to swim at a lake in Connecticut one summer where he was completing his Ph.D. There was some type of floating dock that led to deeper water, way over my little head.

CHAPTER FOUR Bombs, No Shelter

With a lot of coaching and assurance, he stood just beyond the dock and said, "I'm going to stay right here. I won't go anywhere, now push off!"

The water was dark brown and cold. I couldn't even see down a few inches. I was scared but felt pressure to show him I could do it. When I couldn't stall any longer, I reluctantly slid in and began to kick and paddle like a doggie. I might have been successful until I realized he kept stepping deeper and deeper into the water, further, and further away from the dock. Panicking, I took in the first gulps of water instead of air. I was unable to keep my head above the water's surface, kicking and waving my arms frantically. Low on breath, I went under once, and again, now twice. Struggling to get back up I could only see brown. I felt the air and tried to grab it before descending a third time. I couldn't get back up, water coming in through my nose and mouth. I was struggling, hurt, terrified, and angry. I finally felt large, strong hands grab my arm, my body following, as he plunked me down on the dock like a net full of useless seaweed. I was sobbing, stammering, and coughing up nasty lake water through tears.

"What happened?" he kept asking, pretending not to know why I was shaking, laughing under his breath, gaslighting me deeper than I'd gone under. I scampered away seeking soothing from my mom.

As a mature adult on a master's swim team, I wondered why I felt like I'd not be able to get enough air to breathe. It was four years of training before I finally felt comfortable enough in the water for the terror of learning to swim to leave the cells of my being. Decades after the swimming lesson in Connecticut, my dad sent me a belated birthday card. He wrote down some of his fondest memories of me. I treasure this sentimental and kind side of him. On the list, I was a tenacious and brave little swimmer as I was learning and when it got tough, I just kept at it!

He had an odd way of conveying lessons. The same summer as the swimming lesson, my dad was in the final stages of his Ph.D. thesis. The energy around our rental house was very intense. My mom was continually yelling at us to be quiet. Sitting in a rocker on the wrap-around porch, my dad was smoking a white tightly rolled cigarette. I'd not seen him smoke before. I was six years old and curious.

Innocently, I asked, "Daddy what are you doing with that thing in your mouth?"

He lured me over and asked me to put the cigarette between my lips, "Now I want you to breathe in as big as you can," he proceeded, coaching me to take the biggest inhale I possibly could with a big smile on his face.

I was excited to obey. The burning went deep. To this day, I wouldn't even think of inhaling any type of cigarette, an odd gift.

Mistreatment added up to a decrease in my feeling of value and being treasured. I was angry and puzzled yet still yearned for my father's attention and respect. What I learned was to treat myself the same way. Disregarding my needs or belittling them by shutting down with awkward stoicism to get approval seemed ordinary. This lesson was repeated often and hard, rooting deeply. Later, a billboard would come crashing down, rocking my reality so severely I had to awaken.

My father's Ph.D. work concluded. As we were preparing to leave Connecticut to return to our Pennsylvania home, we were at a goodbye event at a picnic ground. My father introduced us to a lady with shoulder-length bottled platinum hair, a paisley pantsuit, and a baby blue corvette. Her vanity plate read 'Suzie.' It felt odd that she and I had the same name. Clearly, I could sense the energy between her and my dad was electric. I felt uncomfortable. Acting shy and looking at his toes my dad seemed as if he was going to hide his head under his armpit. I felt immediate shame when I picked up more of the clear chemistry. I couldn't understand why we were meeting this woman, my mother looking on, frozen. I moved away as quickly as possible to escape the situation. I knew something was off, way off, but tried not to give it too much thought. The tension between my parents was thundering for me. We finally got into our station wagon and pulled away. For long moments there was seething silence between my parents.

"Really, Fred?" my mom asked heatedly, breaking the silence, "Is that what we need to see? Class act!"

Sheepishly and in response my father replied innocently, "I didn't do anything. I don't know what you're implying." And then more deafening and surly quietude.

Regardless of circumstances, I was always trying to reach higher with my dad to impress him. If I brought home a report card with all A's and one B excited to show him, he'd ask, "Susie, why'd you get the B?" And I'd never be sure if he was serious or silly.

A mystified silence was my usual response and then red shame again. The drive for my dad's approval was strong while the reward was always just at the other end of a baited line. I kept going after it. I wanted him to recognize me, see me, and take care of me with a kind, and consistent gentleness.

Some Friday nights during the winter, my dad would take us to the gym at the university where he was a professor, usually with some of our friends in tow. It was around the time *Mary Poppins* had been released. My sister and I walked with our umbrellas open above our heads across campus trying to catch the wind and fly. A large gust of wind came, and I was certain I had lifted off into the air. Belief in magic was so life-affirming.

It was wild fun to tramp on the trampoline, throw an oversized medicine ball toward one of my brothers or try to make a basket on the basketball court across the corridor. It was a special time when we had my dad's attention.

CHAPTER FOUR Bombs, No Shelter

The competition between siblings was encouraged with no time for sensitivity or babying. Pizza would often come afterward, treasured comfort food.

One Friday night we had another professor's wife and her children along with us while her husband was away coaching the college basketball team. She was cruel and castrating to her oldest son, named after her husband, teasing him mercilessly, while glorifying her youngest son who could do no wrong. I could sense clearly the effect it was having on the older boy, crushing him and the empath within me. As we were waiting for everyone to come out of the locker room, I laid into the mom for her behavior, calling her out for her unequal treatment of her boys. The words just kept rolling off my tongue. She stood stock still, speechless, unable to answer or attempt to defend herself. She stood still at the top of the stairwell, while I was shouting from the floor below. I usually didn't speak these truths but this time they came rolling out of my mouth almost uncontrollably. It was becoming more unsafe to demonstrate that kind of sensitivity.

With a college campus across the street and a father who taught there, it was like having a large personal playground. We biked, skateboarded, roller skated, chalked on the chalkboards, played on the tennis court, and ran around the track that looped the football field for hours on a weekend or vacation day. We also tried tricking the vending machines for free food and made big messes in the brand-new microwave.

One of our favorite pastimes was to play in the telephone booth with a folding door to get in and out and a big fat phone book to select numbers for prank calls to random area residents. We'd dial asking, "Is your refrigerator running?" If they answered "yes," we'd scream, "You better go catch it" and erupted into howls of laughter.

My dad was often in the computer center. We loved the confetti created with Cobalt paper punch cards. My dad would save it in a cardboard box for us to play with and we'd have confetti battles in the parking lot. It was hypnotic to watch the green and white perforated paper feeding through the main computer processor taking up most of the room. I loved my father's intelligence, questioning technology, and deducing answers.

As a kid, it was easy to love my dad. He seemed as if he was my lifeline. He always appeared to be the good guy, taking us on adventures, helping us with our bikes, roller skates, or skateboards, and playing with us. He seemed to be the one who was being taken advantage of by a surly, overweight, unstable, and emotionally disturbed wife.

He'd start drinking, alcoholically, early. I'd wake up on a school day to hear the dry-sink door opening downstairs at 7:30 am, a whiskey bottle being uncorked, and the sound of glug, glug, glug as the amber liquid slid down his throat giving him pseudo strength to take on another day. He was almost always inebriated and absent, physically, emotionally, and more often both. He had the proclivity to chase whatever was close by in a skirt without much discretion.

My father's addictions led my mom to take on most of the load of responsibility for five kids in short progression and care for them. Though she would say she loved us, it was apparent she was trapped, and she resented it. There were continual angry verbal assaults aimed at us often instructing us not to have kids because they really mess things up. This may be one of the reasons there are only two blood grandchildren in our family. Obscured was a feeling of being consistently loved, special, and worthy.

My first holy communion was coming up. I was excited in the reception hall at church one Saturday morning for a special session with the parish priest to practice before our ceremonial day. Katie Inlin was there. She was a blonde, blue-eyed angelic child from a family with only two children, both girls. Perfectly groomed and clothed, there was an air of sophistication and glamor about her. Our priest was talking about the crowning of the Blessed Mary during the communion service. He was beginning to describe that part of the service, speaking about who among us would physically crown the Blessed Mary when Dr. Inlin, Katie's dad, appeared through the doorway. He had a smile on his face and was looking proudly at Katie. I knew in an instant it wasn't going to be me doing the crowning. The lovely honor was going to Katie. I sensed immediately there was some sort of payoff Dr. Inlin had made to the church to grab the privilege for his younger daughter and I was envious. In second grade at around seven years of age, I could so clearly see through a setup.

I wanted so much for my own parents to treat me like a coveted and special gift. They could barely keep themselves afloat with the drama their own relationship created: addictions, mental illness, and having five children to raise. I was disappointed yet resigned myself to the circumstance.

Third grade was particularly rough. My dad fell off the roof of the two-story science building while messing around with his latest side interest. He broke his leg and was hospitalized with a blood clot. Oddly, I was sent to the home of his paramour for some semi-burnt toaster pizza while my mom was at the hospital with my dad. I appreciated her kindness and the toaster pizza but was confused trying to figure out why I was with this woman and her children. She had been part of the reason my dad was in his circumstance. I thought silently, *How could my mother send me here with this woman who was with my father when he had the accident?* It felt a little like being introduced to the baby blue Corvette-driving Suzie. My perception of these events was clear though it would really twist my sense of well-being, especially when coupled with the need to pretend everything was fine.

The white wall phone had been ringing loudly before my mother answered. She was on briefly and hung up quickly.

"Get dressed," she ordered, "get your brothers and sister, we've got to get

CHAPTER FOUR Bombs, No Shelter

to the hospital." I wasn't sure why, but that was true of a lot of directives in my family, you just did as told and quickly.

Soon after, we arrived in the hallway of intensive care near the gray and airless nurse's station. We were lined up according to age and told by our mom that our dad may not live. "This may be the last time you will see him," she whispered, mascara dripping down her left cheek nearing the bottom left corner of her mouth. My breath was frozen and unsure. None of us said anything to each other. I mostly looked at the floor sliding the toes of one foot toward the other. What did this mean? What would happen if my dad died? Would we be orphans?

We filed into the hospital room and my dad was of course doing his best to joke with us and make light of his circumstances explaining the blood clot scientifically and why he had to remain still. We all feigned some type of normality in that dense hospital room filled with the trapped scent of spoiling milk, rubbing alcohol, and human sweat. I wondered if he could stay still or if the clot in his blood would travel to his heart and in an explosive beat, he'd be dead. It was more than I was able to compute. I remember going to that familiar place of feeling frozen and breathless knowing I had to be a very good girl, or my father could die. It would be my fault. I blacked out my escalating feelings.

My dad made it through. The blood clot dissolved before it reached a vital organ. And when he did come back home, not long after, there was even more tension than there had been before.

The same year at nine years old, I was diagnosed with Rheumatic Fever. The illness can scar the heart and cause serious damage to the heart valves forcing the organ to overwork when pumping blood. In hindsight, it fits perfectly to have had my heart under fire physically and metaphorically.

My mom came to the hospital every day and often cried softly at the side of my bed. I didn't really understand why. I appreciated the attention being fragile and seriously ill seemed to bring. I intuitively knew I would be fine. In whispers I heard, "she may never walk again" when the doctor came in to visit. I didn't buy it. I wouldn't even let the idea seep very deep into my psyche.

After my mom had left one evening the doctor came by and asked me to get up and see if I could walk around the bed. Gladly, I obeyed, flinging both legs over the side of the bed like a sprite, easily walking the semi-circle. Soon after I was released, having to take a round pink Bicillin pill twice a day until I was eighteen.

While I was hospitalized yet another of our many family dogs committed suicide - with hindsight it seemed like suicide - hit by a car on the road where we lived and put to sleep. Being a dog in our home was not easy and not anywhere near the pampered lifestyle of the dogs I've had in adulthood. I was sad to get that news which was becoming a swirl of blurry blips too chunky to digest.

Dogs were emotional confidants and companions. I felt they clearly understood me and were more compassionate than my siblings and unpredictable parents. Losing them was too much pain for me to process. By ten years of age, my capacity for emotional shutdown was already expanding beyond my years. Putting my head down and just moving on became my way to cope. Comfort and affection felt littered with danger.

Miss Maurer was my third-grade teacher. She was under five feet tall, and that included the measure of her teased-out wide hair, which was at least half a foot high. She was like a little green Martian minus most of the green. A mean green Martian who ate way too many sour balls, sour pickles, and sauerkraut.

That year I thought it would be funny to sign Valentine's Day cards for each of my classmates from "Mr. Nobody." Miss Maurer didn't think it was too funny.

"Who signed their Valentine's Mr. Nobody?" she accusingly asked and proceeded on a witch hunt to discover who the "Mr. Nobody" Valentine's culprit was by examining handwriting.

At first, I didn't understand why she was making a fuss. Her hunt came down between me and Joe Hannah. I flatly denied I was the culprit and Miss Maurer could not exactly decipher which one of us had signed so I was off the hook. The look of astonishment and disgust on his innocent face haunts me.

My parents' rage was intensifying. It was either screaming attacks and objects being thrown or it was an eerie dead quiet, both equally terrifying. I bounced between wanting it to be all over or the absolute dread and fear of my parent's marriage breaking apart. Panic coursed through my body when I thought of being sent away or adopted if something really did happen to my parents. Being separated from my mother and father as well as my siblings was too terrifying to analyze. Yet the reality of my home life was becoming more gruesome to contain.

It became real combat to fend for any scrap of attention chaotically tossed my way from our parents. As siblings, we began to turn on each other. My oldest brother seemed to focus on me as his outlet for abuse and anger. He was going through puberty and began using me as a lab experiment. It was deeply traumatic, and I blacked out most of it until my mid-twenties.

Breathing into hate, anger, and endless competition, while needing to be on guard to try to find any scrap of safety was wearing. In a tumultuous and often brutal home, the foul taste of shame, guilt, and never measuring up felt unjust and continually defeating.

With no safe place to dispose of the pandemonium of emotions, they were passed like a hot potato amongst my siblings and my parents to me and back again. If not in my family it came from the church, school, friends, or worse, the TV.

I tried to radiate light to soothe the balm of what was bad mental and emotional programming. The dark was becoming overpowering. I was more preyed upon, emotionally numb, and shut down by the day. It was harder to keep my friends after I would act out the rage I was feeling. I couldn't hide the dirty shame and confusion inside and out.

Feeling bludgeoned and bloody from the world's initiations, it is hard to grapple with the understanding that I wanted these lessons for my own evolution. I wasn't yet at double-digit birthdays but handling difficult abuse and trauma and trying to hold myself accountable.

Dependent on adults and authority figures, I didn't understand my level of vulnerability. I was becoming more battered and felt painfully unworthy of living.

TOXIC FAMILY

CHAPTER FIVE
BURGEONING BETRAYAL

By the time I was in fifth grade and ten years old, my parent's marriage was unraveling with mighty force. Divorce in our small town was almost unheard of at the time. Acting out in school, calling the teacher names, and swearing became an issue for me. My self-esteem was plummeting while my anger was rising. The principal called my mom in for a meeting. She explained the potential divorce.

That chaotic summer, I was sent to my grandparents in Ohio on a solo trip and welcomed the escape. I loved my grandfather, even after the blanket bonfire five years before, and felt a bond with him. I stayed at their small, neat-as-a-pin, nothing-out-of-place home with my invalid grandmother about half a block from a busy four-lane street called Ridge Road. We always knew when you saw the funeral home on Ridge Road, that it was the sign to turn onto Dartworth Drive. The left turn brought on ominous excitement. My grandparents' house was the third one down the block on the left, white with green shutters.

In the summertime, it was often hot, even with a large blue and white box fan continually running. The carpeting was synthetic and airless. It seemed to be forever, waiting for my grandfather to get home from work. He ran a small ironworks business near downtown Cleveland called Anvil Products. Initially, he hand-crafted church bells and ornamental iron gates. Eventually, he moved to supply machine parts when factory-pressed garden furniture began taking over his hand-forged market.

A short walk to the local library, Lawson's convenience store, or a longer walk to the mall or swimming pool broke up endless boring days. Everything was predictable at my grandparent's, almost militantly so. My grandpa and I would go to the grocery store together on Saturday mornings. He'd place everything in the cart in precise order, like his own home shelves and closets, not a thing was out of place, ever. There were no labels off-center and nothing extraneous or unnecessary was included. Lint balls were promptly picked up by hand from the carpets, failing roses deadheaded and the not-so-faint smell of mothballs was seeping through the closet shelving.

During this visit, I was in the tiny bathroom taking a bath, enjoying the feel of the water and hot breeze with the scent of freshly cut grass coming through the smoked glass window that was slightly open. Suddenly, the doorknob on the bathroom door started to jiggle. I could see the silver ball handle quiver. My breath tightened. The door burst open, and my grandfather entered. Shocked, I tried to cover my body with a square white washcloth the best I could. It seemed like he was in a trance. His eyes were still and almost frozen as he looked down at me. I felt chills of recognition as they were the same slitty eyes I'd seen on my mom in the bathing incident.

"Leave, grandpa!" I said frantically.

Hauntingly, he leaned down toward me, "I only want to help you wash your back, honey," he replied softly.

"No grandpa, I don't want you to," I yelled, looking him straight in the eye with all the strength a very vulnerable and naked ten-year-old could muster. Then I felt it. Something clicked, and the moment stood still. He backed away, silently, and closed the door.

Until I was in adulthood, this event was never mentioned again. For the rest of my stay, I tried to pretend everything was normal, but it wasn't. I shied away and kept to myself, especially when my grandfather was around barely meeting his glances. It was another haunting experience of betrayal I'd bury. Sixteen years later this and more would swivel back up and out of a deeply submerged chamber during a flashback that left me wobbling, unable to use my legs, and grabbing the wall for support.

The feeling of snakes in the foreground and background of my existence was tangible. This latest incident deepened my sense of unease, and my central nervous system amped up another notch.

When I saw, later in life, Greta Gerwig's 2019 feature film version of *Little Women*, there was a scene where Beth March is invited next door to play the prized piano any time she wishes. The instrument belonged to the now-deceased daughter of Mr. Laurence, the owner of the estate. Watching the film, I noticed I became frozen during the scene where Beth quietly wanders over to play.

My body temperature began rising with the heat of fear and shortness of breath. Once in the grand home, Beth sits in solitude playing the piano with gentle ease, subtle joy, and innocence.

Convinced she was marching herself into a traumatic episode, I projected her vulnerability, piercing my soul. As Beth plays, Mr. Laurence is stealing down the stairway listening in from the other side of the wall. My shoulders tightened toward my ears, squeezing my eyes shut. I was feeling the snakes.

None of what I was projecting happened in the movie as the scene was moving forward.

I realized my reaction didn't match the situation of Beth's movie, but rather my own. It was what was playing out in the cellular memory housed not so deep in my own flesh and bone.

These types of flashbacks and PTSD sensations of breathlessness, unwarranted danger, impending doom, and lurking sinister energies have plagued me more than I've allowed my conscious being to realize. Living with them most of my life has made authentic joy and freedom a rare-known luxury. I've experienced a state of hypervigilance, multiplied by anxiety and a need for constant movement.

Somehow, this level of fear was propelling me to excel outside standard systems. Often, taking large risks and working to exhaustion to prove some type of worth or value were essential to find safety.

My dad and several of his students used pickaxes and shovels to dig down through three feet of earth removing the old coal bins in our basement and transforming it into a rec room. This is where I'd watch Barbara Walters on my belly in a bean bag chair on the floor and ferret out some sense of peace in relative obscurity. Watching the opening for the *Million Dollar Movie* on New York's Channel 8, car headlights streaming down Park Avenue caught my attention. One day, I knew I needed to get to New York City. I felt I'd have freedom in that metropolis to pursue the dreams of the person I wanted to manifest. I'd fit in and have an opportunity. New York City emblemized the magical place I'd been seeking, the golden ring. Though scary, I was determined to keep my focus.

The affection and attention in our home came riddled with a string of barter, trauma, and mixed emotions. My mother's hugs felt invasive when they came. Always on her timetable and more for her than for me, stifling with a nasty stench from her nightgown, seconds to smothering in length. From across the room, she'd say, "come here, let me give you a hug." I'd trudge over for the unappealing exchange.

My father was more of an unpredictable force, available when it was good for him. He never once told me he loved me as I was growing up, and I usually was chasing his admiration, falling short, my fragile self-esteem silently languishing into a blackening angry heart.

I'd go to bed early if I could, often by 7:30 pm, knowing I would be woken either by my parents fighting or my mother flipping on the light in my room, ripping the clothes in my closet off their hangers and out of my dresser drawers screaming for things being out of order and a mess.

I remember going to see *Mommy Dearest* in college with my dear friend, Julia. The film depicts Christina Crawford's adoptive mother, Joan, as an abusive and manipulative parent. I was stunned by the similarities. It was the same volatile environment I grew up in, with a very different address.

Whisperings of divorce came again. This time, I was almost relieved. Vicious fighting between my parents late at night made it hard to find rest. The tension was becoming unbearable when my parent's shrill screaming woke me from a deep sleep right outside my bedroom door.

"Fred, please, don't kill me," my mother begged.

I scrambled out of the lower bunk and opened the door to find my mom on her knees, hands folded in prayer, and my dad in a drunken stupor with a kitchen carving knife clenched between his hands above the centerline of his head.

"Sssssttttooooooooooopppppp!" I yelled for as long as I could at the top of my sleepy lungs, and then everything went black. I hit the floor hard.

Not long after that incident, as I was nearing our home on the walk back from school, I saw my father's clothes fly out of the second-story window landing all over our front lawn. I had to look again to be sure I wasn't imagining it. Shirts and pants were hanging off plants and in between the ivy.

My mother was on the second level of the house doing the pitching. As quickly as she was throwing them, I began gathering the clothes and bringing them back into the house. My next youngest brother was helping me. There was no way I wanted my dad to go, who was standing amongst the ivy in silence. I didn't think I could survive my mother's rage solo without a barricade of pseudo-safety.

Dr. Inlin, Katie's dad, came slowly driving down the street gawking out the car window of his gold-colored Barracuda-looking car, taking in the view.

I felt the familiar hot red shame swim into my being whispering, "You know you're unworthy of a stable home life, a mom and dad who love each other, authentic support, and a safe haven."

My dad did leave. He rented a small musty trailer near the Susquehanna River and drove around in an old used Plymouth Valiant station wagon he picked up.

I tried to tell myself divorce was fun. My dad came to school to take me out to lunch and would take me out to dinner with him on occasion, usually at a bar. Finally, I felt special. He was pumping me for information about my mom, but I didn't understand the manipulation. I reveled in the attention.

My mom announced without my father living in the house, we'd now be struggling for money. Her belief solidly fed into my own equation of no man plus house equals impossible financial difficulties. It would take my own seemingly inequitable divorce to recognize and exorcise this rigid belief.

Dance classes came at a heavy discount to support my newly single mom. My friends' families started including me on their outings and trips, including Katie Inlin's. It was hard not to feel less than, somehow defective and odd, yet special at the same time.

My mom was working at a very small 24-hour diner called the Ho-Hum, popular with truckers before she began working steadily at a more upscale family-style restaurant. Rather quickly, she snagged herself a boyfriend, Mr. Graywell, with piercing blue eyes and a soft curl to his red chestnut hair. Those eyes of his had a tinge of the wild in them as if whoever was home was partially vacant. They reminded me of how I'd seen my mom's and my grandpa's eyes. I felt nervous around him and on guard, looking behind his seemingly soft exterior visage.

At Christmas, three out of the five of us had the stomach flu with one bathroom to share. My mom was working a 3 pm to 11 pm shift. Mr. Graywell was taking care of us. We met in the bathroom. I was on my knees hanging over the toilet after just throwing up.

"Are you alright?" he asked gingerly.

I looked into his eyes fixed and staring through me. I took note of my surroundings and tried backing away from him as he neared. Ducking down, I slithered away, making it to safety inside the bedroom I shared with my big sister, slamming the door hard behind me. Breathless with fear and nausea, I threw myself onto my bed drawing the pillow to my stomach for whatever comfort and shielding I could manage.

With Mr. Graywell around, my dad would sneak into our backyard at night to try and spy on my mom. I remember seeing the shadow of his off-white raincoat while he was darting to the back corner of our shed one night. In a twisted way, a feeling of danger and pursuit equaled caring and love in my young and impressionable mind.

By the time I was almost twelve, though my parents were fully divorced for two years, my dad ended up moving back into our home to live with my mother for another five years.

Part of me was relieved to have our family in one piece again while another part of me was leery. I didn't have faith that the buoyancy would last very long, and I knew unpredictable arguing would start up at some soon-to-come future point. I no longer experienced that same feeling of being 'special' in my dad's eyes. Gone were the lunches, dinners, and outings as he began to acclimate back into the family home attempting to curry favor with my mom. Specialness was over, and there would be more walking on crushed glass for everyone.

On the precipice of turning thirteen, I was dusting the jelly cabinet in the dining room when my mother appeared, "You're going to be a REAL problem now!" she jabbed.

I shook off the typical confusion after being handed some cruel sentencing with little reasoning for the unjust charge. Her sole basis for this belief was that I would soon be a teenager.

"I don't know what you mean, mom. I'm having another birthday," I reasoned.

Her mind was firmly planted. Almost as I blew out thirteen candles at the surprise birthday party she lovingly threw for me, she began creating scenarios in which I was the guilty party, the presumption of innocence void, a sacrificial lamb with no acquittal.

The violence between us became more fervent.

Victimization penetrated though I tried to convince her logically her accusations were flawed, assuaging her depression, and helping her realize her beauty and talents. It was a tenuous dynamic, sometimes seemingly successful only leading to a complete collapse, the manipulation thick. At this point, childhood and my connection to my mother were for all respective purposes severed.

Confusion reigned down like a cascading and violent waterfall. Her mood switching became more frequent. She'd be in the middle of prepping, organizing, decorating, or something, spin around, and hit me screaming, "Make yourself useful, Susie, you lazy *itch!"

I began to find it harder to carry the shame, her shame, and I began to fight back. Our flesh met in kicks, slaps, and bruising pinches mostly to my detriment. Hate and blame began to grow like red algae. The pain of bewilderment and paranoia was overwhelming. The fear of retaliation, if I stood up to her illness, grew. And to nurture myself and find kindness and self-compassion became impossible. Unable to hold on to the truth, I shut down tight into a wad of debilitating darkness and rage. My central nervous system was in constant overdrive in fear of attacks.

On the other side was my dad. Before I'd felt a kinship, now he was siding with my mom to avoid being thrown out again. I was feeling the withdrawal losing a co-dependent nightmare brings. He couldn't handle my shift from a young girl to a young woman and began ridiculing and teasing me incessantly about anything that had to do with my femininity. His words were bashing blows and continual - the way I walked, how I ran on the tennis court, my make-up, and my clothes. His rejection ripping through my heart again and again, I began

CHAPTER FIVE Burgeoning Betrayal

to bury it deep within me feigning nothingness, obliterating emotion, and creating a plastic impenetrable sham.

Now I was becoming defenseless. I was slipping into the insanity of our home and turning away from my inner knowing. Standing my ground, not having to defend it, but just standing in my truth was not possible. Having rage projected with no recourse and two parents I could not trust was something I couldn't surmount. Ultimately, sucking it up with a straw, I maintained the belief I was at fault holding a strong desire to transform rage that did not belong to me; I began carrying this density physically in and on my body.

My weight started to become my focus. I would attempt to find control of my reality through food. Faulty attempts to eat in relation to the amount of exercise I was doing to find inner perfection were subtle at first and then grew significantly. My mom's body weight made seismic shifts – up to 210, down to 140, up to 235, and down to 170. She'd eat out of the grocery bags even before we'd make it into the car desperate to find a sliver of peace and simple soothing. It was a huge issue for her and a vulnerable target of ridicule and shame. Fearing my weight would balloon like my mother's was terrifying; simultaneously, I'd see my father staring at my body up and down, ogling me like I was another one of his singled-out prey in a skirt.

The passage to a teenager was difficult.

My mother did everything to either strip self-love, the softness of femininity, and self-care out of my system or did exactly the opposite and smothered me, chastising me for not being kinder to myself. It was a whirlwind of uncertainty and confusion that I was willing to make the best of for all of our sakes.

Mostly, I became mum, stayed out of the house as much as possible, and when I was at home, tried to stay hidden. I focused on what I could achieve which turned into a mission to find how I could be perfect, to somehow get above this madness or better, evaporate.

I wanted understanding, stability, support, and consistency. I wanted peace rather than my mother's illness of tempestuous paranoia and unpredictable rage and my father's predatorial and alcoholic narcissism.

Peppered with this combo was continual sibling violence and jealousy. Competing for the few scraps of attention sparsely doled was my focus. My oldest brother raging with hormones had survived the brutality of our home the longest and was fiercest in acting it out. He has very few memories of growing up. They're mostly blacked out.

One day after school, I made the mistake of using his stereo to play a record I wanted to listen to in his bedroom upstairs. A little while later, he found me downstairs in the living room,

"Don't you ever touch my stuff again," he yelled, grabbing my hair, and proceeding to bash my head against the wall - stars, heat, and black were all that

I could feel and see.

In adulthood, I went to a sound healer who used tuning forks for releasing trauma in my quest for wholeness. During a session, she stunned me, "When did you get a concussion?" she asked.

Though I hated his viciousness, I blamed myself for trespassing. By that point, I didn't bother going to either of my parents for help, internalizing the abuse. A warped sense of responsibility for another's misplaced rage was already normal.

My sister had a friend visiting. They were shooting the BB Gun at a target on the lawn, and I wouldn't leave them alone wanting to join in.

"Let me shoot, let me shoot!" I was begging repeatedly.

Frustrated, after I didn't accept loud and repeated answers of "no," my sister turned and fired, hitting me straight in the navel.

Violence or sarcasm was the standard way of dealing with issues in our family followed by feigning laughter to get through the moment while appearing impervious or roaring back with an attack. We'd received the messaging loud and clear that it was better to appear stoic, vulnerability was treacherous.

Consistent respect, fairness, and integrity were saved for Never Neverland. Scraps of love unveiled were laced with passive-aggressive messaging, *I love you and I hate you, come closer, getaway*. Passing moments of nurturing would shift quickly and there was almost always a price tag. My parents, both equally brilliant, demonstrated a level of intellect that like a covert minefield was hard to detonate.

The *don't do as I do, do as I say* caveat of my father left me wobbling. My mother's continual abusive eruptions added to a place where I couldn't grasp balance. Consistent tools or rules to live by were non-existent. Smothering in some odd affection and attention for some athletic or academic feat or being cruelly rejected and used as a pawn against one of your siblings or a parent was more like the prevailing handbook.

Living this way created incredible anxiety and very little semblance of authentic self-esteem. Food, which had always been my go-to, transformed into an obsession. I wouldn't eat in the morning or at lunch at school. Once I got home from school, ravenous, I'd plow into the kitchen throwing my books down to binge on whatever I could find in the cupboards until I was almost ill. It didn't matter what the combination was – carelessly made Lebanon Bologna sandwiches on white bread with lettuce and mustard, an oversized brandless tub of salty, oily, peanut butter coupled with Nestle's chocolate chips. I'd foist it all down my throat by the spoonful, along with some cold lasagna in one afternoon's folly. At least it would do for twenty minutes to silence the bestial inner dialogue and free-floating fear replicating my mother's behavior.

"Where did the bag of chocolate chips go?" my mother would ask. I'd

CHAPTER FIVE Burgeoning Betrayal

deny I'd eaten or even knew of them. And when my siblings or mother wondered who attacked the leftovers or food in the cabinets, silence again. Then I would be off to dance class for several hours to try and burn it all off, attired not just with tights, leotard, and leg warmers but often 100% PVC plastic sweatpants emulating a sauna, like the high school wrestlers wore to make weight.

Between hormones and overeating, it all caught up with me and that intense self-hate thermometer inside began to soar. My eyes were dull and shadowed by darkened circles, my skin had an odd flat tone. I was a basket of shame continually comparing how my jeans fit and felt and how I looked in them in comparison with my fellow female classmates. I was on that dead ended loop for decades with the insanity of trying to hide discomfort and drown it out with food.

Self-destruction became more of my focus. Training at a Grade A level to hate and abuse myself, competing with my fellows, albeit quietly, and always seeking a bit more leverage for myself was drilled into me. Sneaking around and avoiding real truths were coupled with fear and a sense of mistrust of others.

I knew this was wrong, it wasn't a fit for who I was in my heart, and I wanted out, desperately. I thought that getting out may be the solution. I fantasized often about leaving. It was much easier than the actual reality of it.

Intuitively, I knew eventually I'd head to New York City. I'd get there and find 'home.' But first, I had to live out what was in front of me. Cells of self-encased memories like icicles freeze my spine to think of the circumstances I faced. A brutal inner message of push harder, do better, you are worthless, selfish, bad, and a rotten girl amped up in volume. Jump ahead, yet you deserve to be at the bottom of the pile, were the inner mantras that seemed to taunt me toward insanity, cracking me from the inside out. And if I wasn't emphasizing that mantra, my mother was continually promising me, "You'll end up locked in a psych ward, you crazy spoiled little bi*ch!"

Throughout my life, I would later learn to respect what happened to me and to love that poor, lost, little girl, frightened to her core. The one who had been ladled with shame and abuse, her self-worth and power trained away at a very early age. Repeatedly I'd somehow chosen the road of transformation to bring in peace where peace had been missing rather than embrace the path of destruction demonstrated.

Having no real grounding in my own value, and being battered on multiple levels, I sold myself short repeatedly. Yet even with all the trauma delivered, I was fierce and stable in holding on to the belief that I would survive, that I would 'make it,' that I would be able to transform all I'd faced as a child to find true happiness, internal contentment, and love.

TOXIC FAMILY

CHAPTER SIX
FALLOUT FROM THE FAMILY FRAY

Sophomore year in high school, I heard about the Pennsylvania Governor's School for the Arts. It was a highly competitive summer program for performance arts. A classically trained dancer, I wanted to win a spot. High school students from all over the state auditioned. Stepping up onto the front porch after walking home from school, I got the mail from the mailbox and saw it. It was a letter from the Governor's School organization. Apprehensively, I opened the envelope and unfolded the letter spilling through the verbiage. I had won a scholarship for dance and would be out of our family home to stay on a college campus, fifteen minutes away, for six weeks.

This experience gave me a taste of what living away from home was like, as well as, a fresh new environment. I lost at least fifteen pounds and felt freer and more hopeful. Meeting other teens who seemed more like me helped me feel less isolated. I had the courage to break up with my boyfriend. I always had a string of 'boyfriends' since second grade and Billy Fritz. Their attention was an absolute must for me to feel worthy and acknowledged, an addiction proving difficult for me to break. I was dependent yet tended to confuse love with pity.

The summer program opened new doors and connections for me to think broader and break out of some of the emotional pain I'd experienced up to this point. I was changed. I went back home with renewed strength of spirit determined to keep the wheels going in a healthier direction.

My last two years of high school seemed like *Groundhog Day*, endless and repeating. I was biding time before I could finally escape. Intuitively knowing I'd be in New York City, college would interfere first. I had no real desire to go to college, yet it seemed a mandatory requirement. Even though my father was a college professor I had no idea you could go to school for things like Radio & TV, which were hugely popular then or create my own area of study.

During my junior year of high school, my father moved out of the house for the second time. It wasn't as dramatic. Like most narcissists, he already had his next 'victim' lined up and waiting. I didn't fight it this time. I was too tarnished and tired from trying in the last go-round, and I had mixed feelings about him since maturing into a teen.

By this point, I knew to keep my head down, accept every opportunity not to be at home, and try to avoid my mom and oldest brother at all costs. We rarely had family dinners anymore and there was not much cohesion. Basically, I was on my own and left to fend for myself until some rumored teenage bad behavior caught the attention of my parents. This happened when a friend of theirs whose son or daughter became mixed up with drugs or promiscuous behavior. They feared I would mingle with the wrong crowd. So they would overreact, creating boundaries where there had been none which was confusing.

I was a senior in high school and seventeen. My exit was looming and as far as college, I focused on a very small highly experiential private school in Vermont. It was prestigious and I thought it would be just like the Governor's School for the Arts. I met with an alumnus as the first hoop to jump, charmed her, applied, and was accepted. I assumed that was where I'd be going without looking elsewhere. I didn't explore other options in-depth and was pretty much figuring it out as I went along.

With foresight, my dad urged me to go see the campus of the school where I was accepted. His concern was I would be coming out with student debt if I chose that school. He didn't want to see me in that position. In very late April, we drove five and a half hours for a visit. After a quick on-campus tour, I knew immediately the school was not a fit. I had no other options. It was late in the game. My feelings about going to college and the value of the experience were mixed. I wasn't terribly anxious about my circumstance which was odd as I usually wanted to follow along with the suggested academic program. I felt a little bit of relief actually and surrendered to it.

A friend from my dance school was completing her master's degree at Ohio University. I got in touch with her. She told me to visit the school in

CHAPTER SIX Fallout from the Family Fray

mid-May when they were having auditions, as I was still dancing. I did and won a scholarship. Checkmark, the decision on college was complete with the great benefit of no student debt.

I was relieved to know where I would be going to college but not that excited about the opportunity. I really wanted to get it over with so I could go to New York City and start working. I had no interest in becoming a professional dancer, it was simply all I'd known up to that point. I really loved the business side of the arts and entertainment yet I didn't know how to translate that into 'college curriculum' speak.

In limbo, I was watching time go by before high school graduation and a summer at the Jersey shore to work on an amusement pier. A former student of my father's owned one of the piers that stretched toward the sea. It was in the same shore town where my dad spent his summers growing up and where we went on vacation. He loved that town with all his heart. He'd tell us numerous stories about that time like taking a canoe out into the ocean during a hurricane or working on an ice truck delivering ice for refrigeration to the Boardwalk businesses and restaurants.

"I was in the best shape of my life," he'd say with a mythical dreaminess.

After seventeen years of bombardment, abuse, abominable manipulation, and shrapnel flying with little shelter in sight, the exit tunnel was radiating steps away. It was exhilarating and terrifying at the same time. Of course, I wouldn't express it. I remember vividly wondering how my two younger brothers would fare and felt survivor's guilt knowing I'd be abandoning them soon. It was overwhelming and scary not to know how living on my own outside of my family home would work. Was I prepared?

My childhood left not just deep scars but gaping wounds leading me into a monstrous maze of anxiety and anguish decades into adulthood. Pain and punishment drilled through my neural pathways. Emotionally, I was shut down tight like a drum. My body was retaining proof of the dark energy I was living through, inflamed, with a contained and sullen smile plastered on my face, my eyes, sad, still, and dim. I was raised to mistrust, compete, defend, hate, and second-guess myself before questioning others. I was boundaryless.

Going on to a new venture, I chose not to focus on fear. There was no turning back. I had to propel myself forward. My confidence was a heavenly gift, and when I waivered, I'd think back to all those times I sat alone, crying in my bottom bunk bed from some traumatic incident cementing why I had to leave.

Ready or not, I packed my things and prepared for a new way of life.

TOXIC FAMILY

CHAPTER SEVEN
A PATH OUT OF THE JUNGLE

A few months later, my high school graduation ceremony was on a Friday night in early June. By 7:45 am Saturday morning, I was packed and getting into my dad's car heading for a job at the Jersey Shore. My mom was still sleeping as were my brothers. Goodbyes didn't seem necessary.

As a gaping empath with few boundaries intact, I was a funnel for the woes, terror, and odd fantasies of others. A plaything wide-open, accustomed to conditional love, neglect, and rejection. Being undervalued, betrayed, and abandoned, was standard. Most often I was expecting to be punished, humiliated, and judged as the problem. It came with the territory of being subject to overt mind fluffing and inhaling blame.

If not thrust upon me, I was trained to treat myself in this very same way. Critical self-judgment and an impossible set of standards to receive self-acknowledgment and acceptance plagued me. My inner dialogue had a cadence built toward self-annihilation. "Don't do that, why would you say that, how could you eat all that, what do you think that person thinks of you, you better not be late, you better clean up that mess," and on it went at a frenetic pace.

My knee-jerk reaction to gain acceptance was to size up what I projected someone wanted of me and deliver it. My needs were irrelevant. My central nervous system was impounded. I didn't pause long enough to decide whether I wanted salad or pasta for dinner or if I wanted to go on a training run or rest. I was obsessed with what I thought I might need for my immediate survival, security, and safety which often was outside approval. Breathing and checking in with myself as to how I felt and what I needed were too painful to consider and could lead to rejection and abandonment.

Prepared with war tactics, a dog-eat-dog mentality, and a salty twist of measured kindness, self-hatred, and shame, off I launched into the world. I was excited to escape my home, yet dreading the unknown. It was a summer of transition with my sister and a few of her college coeds as roommates at the shore in Wildwood, NJ.

I loved walking the long cracked concrete sidewalks in my rubber flip-flops. I could feel the joy of beachgoers who walked the same route. Going down to the beach each day, and watching the families and lovers and friends and worried mothers became a comforting routine. I baked my body, taking my small lounge chair right into the water and slipping my feet into the sea. Sun, sand, the rolling regularity of the waves, and seagulls soaring were easing some of my self-defeating inner chatter. Nature was healing.

The opportunity to be a regular at the beach during the day and ride my bike to the boardwalk for work each night was just the balm I needed. It was comforting to have my big sister around though we were mostly passing ships. It was also my first experience in a bar, underage, learning to drink Tootsie Rolls, while I'd rather have had the real candy instead.

I realized quickly that alcohol seemed to ease my anxieties of feeling out of place, less than, and a loner, though I was leery of the intoxicant. Intuitively, I knew it would not be my answer. When I did drink, it was always to escape a feeling of unease within myself, not a good sign.

The smells and flashing lights of the Boardwalk gave me a feeling of excitement. Humidity mixed with the salty sea breeze continued to relax me. I had my future alma mater, Ohio University (OU), t-shirt on under my amusement pier uniform when a guy with a camera hanging from his shoulder and a funny multi-colored cap on his head, running a game on the Boardwalk stopped me.

"Hey, I'm going to OU this Fall," he shouted, enthusiastically.

I turned around and we spoke briefly. He was from Delaware and was going to OU for photojournalism. He was really looking forward to going to college, super excited! I didn't share his ebullience, though we became friends. Later, at school, he would introduce me to my beloved college boyfriend, as well as become a Pulitzer Prize-winning photojournalist.

After work one night and with co-workers from the amusement pier, we piled into a car and rode to Atlantic City where the very first legal casino outside of Nevada, was opening. I'd never been to a casino before. It was amazing to be ushered into what felt like real glitz and glam with thick red carpets and crystal chandeliers. It was hard not to gawk in front of college boys from Delaware that seemed like shiny objects but turned out to be nothing short of tarnished scum.

I had minimal filters.

How could I receive or treat myself with dignity and respect after the abuse and mind-fluffing of the years of my youth? It only made me an eager people pleaser to garner any kind of attention and receive what seemed like love. What I didn't realize was every bit of my experience was in a specific plan of

CHAPTER SEVEN A Path Out of the Jungle

learning assignments for this lifetime.

My continual path of internal thinking went something like this: *I do not see the anxiety in you, yet I know the anxiety in me. Can you help me escape this loop? Will you be the one to help me ease out of the brutal matrix of this nasty unending polarity I'm struggling with night and day? Will you be my rescuer? I'll be a good girl! You won't be sorry!*

With this toxicity coursing through my veins, how could I enter life as a pseudo-adult and navigate the road ahead with integrity and self-respect? What I was more concerned about knowing was how to release the pulse of fear continually running on a loop with resounding messaging that I was not good enough and unsafe. As it was in my family home, I did not have a clue about how to find comfort, authentic belonging, and trust. I was leveled with apprehension and had few tools for living in a healthy way.

My late teens and early twenties became filled with a different pain, being aware of not knowing who I was inside. Shapeshifting on a dime depending on who I was surrounded by like some sort of social chameleon and feeling out of sorts, false, and vulnerable was a constant.

All of the spontaneous battles with my mother kept me at an anxious tipping point. Though unaware, one of the skills I learned to try and find safety was reading the person with whom I was engaging. Subtly, I'd adapt to their specific temperament and rhythm. It was a survival technique I learned to hone to perfection. Many people I knew felt I was their close friend when really I was keeping them at arm's length. I landed in college by Fall like a fawn who'd lost its mother in a forest fire. My father drove me from the Jersey shore to the school and bought me the proverbial supplies. I remember him looking at me as he prepared to leave, guilt-stricken panic on his face.

"Are you sure you have everything you think you need?" he asked for the third time.

I could clearly read his mind as he silently pondered if he had prepared me enough for this next portion of my life. I put on a good show from the exterior to assuage his fears.

"Oh yes, I'm fine," I replied, eating his concern.

My first term as a college freshman was filled with loneliness and longing for the home I couldn't wait to escape. It took me by complete surprise and seemed nonsensical having continually dreamed of getting out. Nonetheless, it was pervasive.

I was in the fine art department as a dance major and did not fit in with the artsy, way-out, dress everyday like it was Halloween and from a thrift shop, non-linear crowd. The answer to finding balance was to pledge the Greek life as a Pi Phi, a popular national sorority, with a posh, two-story white mansion complete with blonde, blue-eyed pledges roaming the wrap-around porch.

Teas at frat houses, hair in curlers all-day wearing shocking pink and green sweaters, Docksiders, and hoodies with Greek lettering cracking gum with all my might really didn't gel with me as it did my sorority sisters. I wanted to find my safe place but felt on the outside edge of a tight circle once again. When it came to feel as if I belonged as a member of the Dance Department, walking on upright nail beds, jumping from ladders with green dye in my bangs, and reeking of garlic with long black hair growing from my armpits was a miss too.

I was lost. I felt vulnerable, ashamed, and defective.

I tried going to church for soothing and connection since that's what I knew growing up, but it seemed completely hypocritical. I gave up quickly in favor of isolating myself to binge on candy, cookies, or carbs to assuage the familiar feelings of anxiety and fear, standing out as a misfit in a sea of students. Eventually, alcohol moved from a side dish to the main one.

During my sophomore year in college, an alumna came through giving a talk about what she did in NYC managing modern dance companies and performance artists. It sounded interesting, she was in the city I knew I wanted to live in one day and her career mixed my love for the arts with business. I clearly knew I didn't want to be a professional dancer. Working at the Jersey Shore that summer, I wrote to her one afternoon from the beach asking for an internship with her firm for the following summer, a year later. She wrote back promptly asking me to come to New York that Winter during my junior year. They were managing their very first Broadway season for a major client and needed help.

The Dance Department at my University was not supportive of internships outside of performing with well-known professional dance companies like Alvin Ailey, Paul Taylor, Twyla Tharp, or Merce Cunningham. The focus was to keep students on the predefined school track with no deviations.

The internship I was suggesting would be in the business side of the arts. Relatively unknown within the school at the time, I had to present my case to the head of the Dance Department on why I wanted this internship. We discussed how it may change my coursework upon my return, adding a series of business courses. I was thrilled at the idea of the shift. It felt like a much better fit. With convincing, the department head took the bait and agreed, though, that wasn't the end of the process.

After jumping the hoop with the Head of the Dance Department, I was instructed to make my way to the Dean of the School of Fine Art. His daughter, Maya Lin, had just won the job of creating the Vietnam War Memorial in Washington D.C. The Dean's office seemed like a high-end museum with artifacts and beautifully framed artworks. He was quietly dignified in a navy suit, starched white shirt, and tie. He spoke softly, looking at me through round horned-rimmed glasses and recessed low lighting setting the tone of the room. He seemed not to understand why I was in his office.

CHAPTER SEVEN A Path Out of the Jungle

"Oh, you are from the Department of Dance…interesting"… he murmured.

I pressed my feet down through the flooring for reassurance. Intuiting, he was not quite sure why I was presenting myself, I began explaining the reason for my visit. Wheels were turning inside his head. I could feel it and I could read his thoughts. Ultimately, he said yes to the new plan and I breathed a sigh of relief. I'd come to know that sigh well. The path I carved became the template of a program in Arts Management. I had a habit of blazing trails without realizing why or what I was doing. I also had a custom of jumping before I measured all angles. The reality of going to New York City as a nineteen-year-old felt scary, even though it had been a goal since childhood. Like leaving my hometown to work at the Jersey Shore, I chose to put my head down, shove my fears aside, and take the opportunity.

My initial landing pad for the internship in New York was Parsippany, New Jersey at my sister's apartment, on her roommate's couch. I was so grateful she was taking me in again and softening another transition. From her apartment, it was a fifteen-minute walk to the bus stop and a forty-minute ride into the city. I felt small and nervous waiting for the bus in the gloomy January frigid air wondering if I was in the wrong place for the bus stop. Soon enough, a lumbering diesel-guzzling extra-wide Trailways bus pulled into the stop. I hopped up the stairs hoping I had the right fare and found my way through the narrow aisle to a free seat avoiding eye contact with the other passengers.

I watched every stop we made wondering when we'd see the famous New York City skyline. And then it came. From the Battery to Harlem, you could see it all off the Hudson River as we rounded a wide semi-circle leading into the Lincoln Tunnel the bus shifting left to right as the driver negotiated that wide and long turn. I loved seeing the city this way. I marveled at the fact I was now working and eventually would be living here, years after dreaming it.

The interior of the tunnel was quiet, subway tile barely lit. The drive through the tunnel seemed long and I tried not to wonder what would happen if river water came streaming through the structure. Suddenly the light of day was back as we made our way into the rear entrance of the Port Authority terminal. We pulled into the berth with a loud 'chushhhhhh' sound and a final jerk as the bus came to a halt. Waiting for my turn, I stepped off the bus into an exhaust-heavy outer station. A murky walk-through of Port Authority came next followed by descending steps leading down into the subway. I felt grown up and like an insider waiting for the 1, 2, or 3 train and another subway ride up 14th street on the L train to get to the arts management office on Union Square. I kept checking the signs compulsively and train directions to be sure I was following the proper path. Anxious, I decided to get up and out after taking the number 1 train to walk the wide blocks of 14th Street and east to my destination. The neighborhood was grimy, crime-infested, riddled with addicts, and more than a bit sleazy. It was all part of the excitement of working in the city.

The company I was interning with was housed in a rundown office building that had decades of wear worn into the walls. It was adjacent to Union Square Park pre–farmers market and sheik gentrification. It was thrilling to finally be working in New York City. Though 14th Street, with illegal designer knock-offs being hawked and three card monte shell games hustling, was frightening I was still thrilled to be walking the city street. I learned later some inhabitants wouldn't dare venture below 14th Street and others wouldn't go above it. The air reeked of burnt chestnuts and searing meat from the vendors who ran push carts for syndicates.

There was a Greek coffee shop next to the building entry where I would be working and a small newsstand just inside. It must have been a glamorous building at one point but that was long ago. Riding up the elevator seemed a bit treacherous. It was overcrowded and made odd mini-halting movements and creaking noises. I held my breath. The doors finally opened on the floor to the office of Arts Arcadia. I saw the sign for the management firm had been stenciled on the smudged patterned glass door down the hallway. This was my very first professional office setting in New York City, and I was apprehensive. I knocked. Lucinda Dobbins, the OU alumna, and one of three partners of the management office opened the door. She welcomed me with a smile dotted with deep dimples. She was short and spunky with self-confidence glowing through her warm persona. It almost seemed she was play-acting as a grown-up.

In the single room with drab and dirty linoleum tiles and fading walls, you could hear the city bustle below and see the treetops of Union Square Park out of the grimy, rattling glass windows.

Adelaid, partner number two, wasn't yet in; she was often a late arrival radiating heavy angst and confusion. Margaret, partner number three, was already chain-smoking hunched over her desk, slovenly with greasy hair and dirt under her tobacco-stained fingernails finishing a bagel with cream cheese slithering out the sides between puffs on a Marlboro cigarette.

Almost instantly I began learning about grown-up professional life and what arts managers do, mostly worry, argue, and gossip about their clients. Margaret and Lucinda began discussing how I would best be put to work.

A few weeks into the internship came the planned day for me to move out of my sister's apartment and into the city for the remainder of my three months of interning. I set out on a freezing blustery Sunday afternoon walking carefully with heavy suitcases, minus wheels, to the bus stop. Leaving the pseudo safety of the New Jersey suburb and my sister was intimidating even though it was a planned and temporary stay. I was acclimating to the city having worked there for several weeks. I felt alone, vulnerable, and at risk, yet was determined to

CHAPTER SEVEN A Path Out of the Jungle

plunge ahead.

It was icy-cold, and the wind was so fierce as I trudged up the dirty subway stairs in the dark that my oversized suitcases blew back in my hands putting heavy pressure on my wrists which I thought might break. It taught me to pack light and my belongings to this day are relatively few. I'd never even thought of the luxury of taking a cab from Port Authority to the apartment where I was staying. And I wouldn't ask my sister for a car ride to the bus stop. It wasn't in my vocabulary.

Walking many blocks through the West Village, I was not sure I was taking the most direct route from the subway stop to the temporary sublet Margaret, the partner in the arts management firm, offered. She was going out on tour with one of the dance companies represented by the firm. I was to take care of her cats, which later I was grateful for on multiple accounts.

After climbing four flights of stairs, with the oversized heavy suitcases in each hand, I found the apartment door and struggled with the key. I'd been warned the key was difficult. By now it was completely dark out and the wind was howling. I didn't want to have to retrace my steps. Sweating from nerves, and after a lot of jiggling, finally, the lock cooperated, and with a click, I entered. This was my first apartment to myself. The door slammed shut, sealing me in. There was a long steel rod to prop into the lock and a green-painted footprint smudged on the back of the door.

Here I was, biting back the shock. I did love the exposed brick wall and lace curtains over two windows with a view into the brick wall of the next building. Barely twenty years old I was now living in Greenwich Village in New York City on my own. I was amazed, nervous, and lonely, yet I knew, finally, this was where I was supposed to be.

TOXIC FAMILY

CHAPTER EIGHT
MOVING FORWARD

As I started to unpack, I saw something scurry out of my peripheral vision. It was a large brown bug and I screamed. Not one but many were fleeing with my intrusion. I'd never seen bugs like these before and it turned out those bugs were crawling in every nook and cranny of the studio apartment. I was afraid to unpack my suitcases. Annoyed and scared, I grabbed the keys and went back down four flights of stairs, out onto the dark streets, and found a local mini-market.

There was a short dark-haired man behind a smeared and scarred plexiglass shield to whom I explained, "Brown bugs with antennae are crawling everywhere in my apartment!"

After a question or two, he patiently explained what I'd seen. Omnivorous cockroaches like to eat just about anything with starch, sugar, grease, or meat and they multiply easily. He offered boric acid in bait trays.

What had I gotten myself into? I wondered as I trudged back to the building. Climbing the four flights of stairs again, arriving breathless inside the apartment, I quickly laid the trays down and began to thoroughly clean the apartment. One thing I learned growing up was how to clean. And boy did I. Roaches freaked me out!

I was wet behind the ears, though I did have a wonderful sense of daring and adventure instilled by my father. I listened, learned, and was willing to take chances. New York had long been a dream and here I was fulfilling it. Though I would not have given myself credit at the time, I was brave. Longingly, I wished my sister or parents would have checked in to see how I was doing.

My work during the internship with the arts management company was mostly spent creating a publicity department and servicing tours of multiple dance companies and performance artists. I also was learning about fundraising for the arts and getting around Manhattan on $80 a week.

I'd walk everywhere which was the best way I could get to know New York City. There was a sense of freedom mixed with a floating danger that was attractive. When I splurged, I loved the coffee in blue and white paper cups with Greek figures printed on them, bagels with a 'schmear', and oversized slices of pizza to walk away with on what quickly became greasy paper plates.

Meeting whom I perceived as high-powered executives on the artists' Board of Directors and multimedia artists who were in esoteric art books was exhilarating. Venturing down to the largely vacant and loft-filled Soho and Tribeca seemed on the verge of life-threatening. The cavernous and empty cobblestone streets with an occasional Artisan restaurant seemed eerily spooky. My heeled shoes and light woolen coat weren't a match for the environment.

Crossing into St. Mark's Place in the East Village was intimidating. I stumbled upon the area during one of my exploratory walks across town. Punk rockers, poets, addicts, and eclectic performance artists manifested like a circus sideshow before it was the trend. Digging my heel into the pavement half a block in, I spun around as fast as I could, desperate to put distance between myself and this exotic and seemingly dangerous place. Piercings, shocking pink hair, and a guy walking around in simply nothing but an American Flag, were way over the top for me. Later I would get to know that guy who'd been walking around in the flag. It was Richard Hell, a punk rocker who had a band called Richard Hell and the Voidoids.

I loved the allure and magic I felt in New York City. It was crowded but there was still some room to breathe. There were a lot of creatives able to afford housing downtown which meant random chance happenings coupled with an air of mystique. I had no urge to get back to college and the theoretical after experiencing the practical. It seemed a useless thing of the past at this present point. I loved the whiff of what felt like an adventure, and the freedom of new experiences.

My apartment sublet was up after six weeks. The partner in the firm was grateful. Her apartment was cleaner than she had left it and free of cockroaches. I was fearful of change having made her apartment my own. A familiar feeling of impending doom and rejection began to swirl around me.

A choreographer represented by the management company where I was interning had a couch in her Tribeca loft near the Battery and was open to an additional roommate. She had several, each with its own door to close. She was on a high after meeting her young and brilliant composer beau who was oozing creativity and writing compositions to match the movement she was constantly creating. The timing was perfect. I got an inside look at how other young twenty-somethings were negotiating city life for the final few weeks of my internship.

There was comradery and tension at the same time. Living in a Tribeca

CHAPTER EIGHT Moving Forward

loft near the Battery was a much different experience than living alone in Greenwich Village. The buildings were cavernous, and the streets narrow, winding, and empty after 7 pm and during the weekends. It felt more as if we were Manhattan's homesteaders. One of the roommates was a former dancer studying to become an animator. She was tiny and cat-like with piercing features. She seemed warm yet distant at the same time. She was curious about my position with the management firm and my life as a college student back in Ohio. Another roommate, Gigi, was making money as a Go-Go dancer in Brooklyn. She had a high-pitched doll-like voice, and a strong east coast accent, and was prone to emotional outbursts sobbing and lamenting the difficulties of her life.

"Whatever you do, collect your money upfront if you take up dancing in clubs, it's a nasty gig!" she'd relay.

In this section of the city, I was exposed to unique artists like Paul Zaloom, a *Pee-Wee's Playhouse* meets Mr. Wizard puppeteer, performance artist, and political satirist best known for playing the character Beakman on the television show *Beakman's World*. At the time he'd put together impromptu shows in his loft and try out new material. It was always with creativity that he found art pieces from bits of plumbing to use to enliven his puppets and materialize a zany form of fun genius. Old humidifiers would collide with spigots manifesting amazing characters. Spaulding Gray and Eric Bogosian also lived in the area. I'd see Spaulding walking with the wind blowing back his black wool coat ends, head down in deep thought, scarf loosely wrapped around his neck. Eric Bogosian's then-girlfriend who would later become his wife, Jo Bonney, came in for meetings at the management firm earning a wage with her graphic design ability. Always dressed in black she was quiet, her Australian accent thick and I was intrigued by her mysterious personality. She'd listen to the partners and their ideas about graphic design for client projects and then quietly add a few bits of her own wisdom which brought incredible dimension and life through the work. She was mesmerizing.

With mixed feelings, I headed back to school. I felt empowered with a clearer perspective returning to campus, yet confused as to the necessity of further study. The arts management company invited me back for the summer, and I jumped at the chance. This time my college boyfriend came along. He did time as an intern with a twenty-four-hour news upstart owned by a maverick from Atlanta named Ted Turner. This experience was a real taste of what I perceived to be the grown-up world, living with my boyfriend in a Chelsea loft and exploring the excitement of the city together. I remember early on, he called me at work during the day and I was shocked. Rigid and compartmentalized when working, I was generally completely focused on the task at hand. He was calling just to check in, and though I had longed for that kind of attention, it was foreign to me. Rejecting any kind of sweetness to the call, I quickly muttered we'd talk when we were back at home and hung up with efficiency. I was programmed to believe work was 'work' with no time for personal anything. It was years later that I realized that was an odd response to a sweet and loving gesture. I had more than a few of those behaviors that would seep out attempting to shed some light on new behaviors that could lead to more of a connected, loving, and gentle way to be toward myself and others.

Returning for my senior year of college saw my alcoholism blossom. There was something inside of me burgeoning to break free. I was jealous that I was not the type of a sorority girl, coveted and fussed over by well-to-do family members, reminiscent of Kelly Inlin and a thru line that would follow me. I was tired of towing some invisible line of allegiance. Though proud of my capability to go off on my own and survive in one of the world's largest cities, I also resented it. I wanted someone to step in and give me ladles of protection and care or express concern for my safety like I saw in some of my sorority sisters and their families. I envied and resented it at the same time.

Alcoholic traits picked up – low tolerance for frustration, non-conformity, and impulsivity. I broke up with my longtime boyfriend and started having an affair with a married hairdresser. I was also becoming more of a regular at happy hour and seats at the bar were familiar friends. Toward the end of the year, I was hiding in my closet from one of my Dance Department Professors who physically came looking for me when I failed to show up for mandatory tech crew duty. I thought it was odd to be hiding in my closet but blacked out the self-doubt and shame by eating most of the food and snacks my roommate received from her family back home. These were red flags I left unnoted. By nature, I was a 'good' girl wanting only to please. My urge for rebellion was mounting.

After coming back from yet another happy hour in a blackout, leaving my books sprawled in the hallway and the door to my room open while I lay passed out on the bed, my sorority sisters tried to ensnare me into a discussion about my drinking. There was a group of students becoming active in Mothers Against Drunk Driving (MADD) which was popping up on college campuses across the country. I would have none of it and was steeped in denial. If they thought I had a problem, they didn't grow up as I did. My father's drinking made mine civil by comparison. All I could care about was that I was getting out of college soon and heading to New York to stay, finally.

I was offered a full-time job with the same arts management firm I interned with, but I wanted to work uptown in a fancy skyscraper handling more mainstream entertainment. Knowing no one in that arena, I took my usual route and asked enough people I knew who they might know or who friends of theirs might know. Those networking questions ultimately led me to a job interview in a glitzy skyscraper with the flashy global talent agency, ICM, short for International Creative Management, where I was to receive my basic combat boot training.

Joe Caan interviewed me. He thought I was a nice Jewish girl because of my last name, and I wasn't going to correct him.

Looking at me over his reading glasses, he told me "We'd like for you to start as an assistant for two of our sales agents who book tours for artists."

I was thrilled to oblige.

My married hairdresser had driven me into the city for the interview. He was trying to fulfill a fantasy of working for Kenneth – a high-end salon Jackie O, Brooke Astor, Audrey Hepburn, and Happy Rockefeller frequented. Ultimately, he chickened out and went back to Ohio and to his devoted wife with his hillbilly tail between his legs. Another unrecognized blessing that drifted my way.

It was time to move into the city and I found myself, again, on another life-changing car ride with my father. He had that same guilty and worried look in his eye dropping me off in Greenwich Village as he had dropped me off at college. As was typical, I noted his discomfort and began to take care of it assuring him I'd be fine. I knew regardless of the lack of consistency and challenges of my upbringing, I was determined to make it and he'd done the best he could.

TOXIC FAMILY

CHAPTER 9
NEW YORK, NY

In New York full-time, solo with no boyfriend in tow, it seemed I'd met an elusive goal. I was fortunate a roommate from the loft experience offered to share her new small studio apartment in Greenwich Village until I got on my feet and found a place.

She helped me up and out within three weeks, which was two and a half weeks too long. Her patience was short. She was combing the *Village Voice* for apartment rentals and shares on my behalf. The city summer was hot, and the studio apartment had no air conditioning.

"My friend from dance class is looking for a roommate," she announced. I was like a lost lamb trying to learn the ropes in my new job and ferreting my way through the city above 14th Street. During my internship places to stay had been found for me and I wasn't awake enough yet to find a place on my own. Once it dawned on me how much pressure I was adding to my friend's lifestyle I was ashamed.

At my roommate's suggestion, I ended up renting the bedroom portion of a one-bedroom apartment on the Upper West Side of Manhattan. Sharon, my new landlord, was a classically trained ballet dancer from a small town in Northern California who slept on a mattress in the corner on the floor of the open living room and kitchen area, covered with purple and blue paisley batik prints. She seemed exotic. She had very long shiny dark hair and oyster-white skin. She used natural health products like Aubrey Rose Water Body Wash, and Tom's Toothpaste and ate only organic foods. She drank cappuccino at Café La Fortuna. I didn't really understand what a cappuccino was at that time and had never gotten into organic oils, toothpaste, or vegetables. She walked like a ballerina, her feet turned out like a duck and was always fighting off the urge to down a pint of Coffee Häagen-Dazs ice cream while complaining about waiting tables in-between fourteen-day clay fasts.

Walking through Central Park on my way to work, gazing at the majestic world-famous skyline, I was proud to be in the great city that was my fantasy, yet feeling vulnerable and alone. It reminded me of all the days walking the long distance to elementary school enjoying the walk yet a little anxious about the situation. I was happy and nervous at the same time. An inner tension was embedded.

My judgments, fear, and anxiety haunted me. There was a constant internal muttering to do more, be more, and excel, coupled with a continual self-whipping over never measuring up. The seemingly programmed mantra pattered continually like a long and soggy rain inside my brain.

For exercise, I started running in Central Park. I met up with Fred Lebow and the New York Road Runners Club. Quickly running a mile loop turned into Marathon training with my focus on finishing the famed New York City Marathon. Compulsivity was a natural undercurrent after being raised in dysfunction. Reaching harsh and measured goals replaced natural inner safety. Along with running, I started working out at one of the first high-end boutique fitness centers, NY Health and Racquet Club. I loved Marta, the Puerto Rican locker room attendant. She had glowing soft caramel skin and dark lustrous hair, her lips painted a reddish pink.

She would calmly open locker after locker in an even meditative state, delivering a fresh towel with peace and calm no matter how many spoiled, young urban professionals were shouting, "Marta, I need a towel. Marta my locker, please open it for me!"

I found a pace and slid into the social sphere.

At ICM, I started in the classical division working with globally renowned classical musicians like Isaac Stern, Itzhak Perlman, and Yo-Yo Ma. I longed to make my way upstairs where mega-talent agents for mainstream artists were housed. Sam Cohn who was famous himself for eating tissues like they were fruit roll-ups was representing Woody Allen. Sue Mengers was the responsible agent for Barbara Streisand, Faye Dunaway, and Steve McQueen. Daniel, my fellow marathoning friend, and recent Vassar grad doing his time in the ICM mailroom was my conduit for information on what it was like on the hallowed 18th floor.

For now, I took in as much information as I could and added side jobs like typing the rabbinical thesis for Isaac Stern's daughter, simultaneously learning to eat chicken liver, and pretending to like it in the sprawling Stern family apartment on Central Park West. I was making friends and influencing Vera, Isaac's wife, with my typing speed.

I finally heard a rumor through my marathoning mailroom friend, who would later open his own successful literary agency, that the head of the celebrity

CHAPTER NINE New York, NY

commercial division was looking for an assistant. I was thrilled and contacted HR right away.

Once I received a green light to interview for the open position, I snuck upstairs during my lunch hour on the appointed day and did my best to assure the agent in need I was right for the job. When I came back from the interview, I found all my belongings packed into a beaten-up cardboard box on top of my desk.

My then-boss, who was a very high-powered agent in the classical music world but a miserable raging bull who went through assistants like water called me into her office, "I hope you got the job; you're fired!" she said bluntly.

I got the job.

The very next week, I was floating on air riding all the way up to the 18th floor. I was so excited to be entering the middle bank of elevators that didn't even stop on the first ten floors. I hung onto every word my new boss had to say. I was yearning to learn the business and get off the assistant desk. Agents almost always closed their doors when real work was done. I hated being an assistant. I hated serving. I'd had too much of that in my childhood.

Much to my surprise, it wasn't long before my new boss told me he was leaving. After years with ICM, he would be forming his own agency doing the same thing he'd done, making deals for celebrities to do commercials. He asked me to join him, and I bit right away. I knew this would be a real chance to learn more than taking messages and typing memos. It was just me and him off the Avenue of Americas on 55th Street in a small studio apartment near all of the large globally known talent agencies.

We worked with no walls, I heard all the negotiations, and I would have never had that opportunity at ICM. I met talents like Stiller and Meara who sent great Christmas gifts, and Richard Simmons who bounced by one day to entertain us like a spark plug from planet X. I also met high-powered managers like George Shapiro who was working with a young comic named Jerry Seinfeld, and George Wallach whose client was the winner of that year's Olympic decathlon, and on a box of Wheaties, known then as Bruce Jenner.

Not so fun was the fact that I was privy to a stream of actresses my boss would schedule for 'testing.' I would be asked to disappear. It was slimy and began to mark darker times for me. I was becoming more isolated, and my drinking was escalating. I felt less comfortable with myself and was encouraged to drink more to fit in with the crowd I found myself surrounded by. Intuitively, I knew alcohol and I were not a good fit, especially considering my upbringing and the degree to which the illness ravaged generations of my family. Something was truly off the day I took a slug from the wine bottle in the fridge at work to discuss more responsibility and a raise. This was a definite deep red flag from that not-so-subtle voice inside. It got my attention.

My first drug of choice was always food, but alcohol began to catch up. It seemed like a close friend. I couldn't come to terms with the thought of giving it up. I didn't know how to meet someone, have a conversation, or go to a party without alcohol involved. The almost immediate self-acceptance and relief from an internal stream of bludgeoning after a chug of intoxicant were alluring until it started to get in my way.

The goals I imagined were becoming more distant. The people I began to associate with were colder, seedier, and fair-weather friends. I now needed alcohol to boost my confidence. I was in a very emotionally abusive relationship and couldn't find my way out. I'd escape and then be lured right back in. It echoed the relationship my parents demonstrated. I didn't understand why my willpower couldn't break that chain and why walking Manhattan streets required a Walkman, headphones, and very dark sunglasses. My skin felt razor thin as if it would crack open at any moment and my eyes were dark with deep brown circles underneath. If someone brushed past me on the subway or while walking on a crowded avenue, I thought I would crumble. Anxiety in the back of my throat was like a vise and becoming more difficult to assuage.

Lying was just as easy as telling the truth. I was having a difficult time keeping straight what story I'd told to whom and most of all knew I was lying to myself. There was a lot of drama I would continually create. The dynamics of my life felt familiar, they were becoming more and more like my childhood home.

I caught on quickly to the understanding something was not working in my life, and I was bravely willing to face it. Luckily, I was led to help and a way of living that offered a firm foundation adding tools for healthy living I was missing.

A friend from my gym slipped me the number of a therapist friend of hers who had been helpful. While grateful for a pathway to help, I also was embarrassed to think I needed to consult a therapist. Woody Allen movies had a bit to do with me re-thinking therapy as chic. I dialed the number and made an appointment to take the bus to the Upper East Side, where I hardly ever ventured. As in the sorority house, I didn't feel at home on the Upper East Side of Manhattan. It seemed that's where all the privileged, well-cared-for 'proper' people lived. I felt I missed those standards. It was a faulty belief system running deep.

The bus ride uptown was tough. Packed on a hot October afternoon, anxiety was coursing through my body. It felt like each side of the bus was squeezing in toward me, nearby passengers infringing on what little space I had, siphoning my oxygen.

I fought off the haunting internal voices of my mom accusing me of being crazy, "You'll end up in an insane asylum you spoiled rotten b%tch!"

I was trained to keep up appearances, be tough, and never appear weak by expressing feelings and emotions. Exposing them to someone I would

CHAPTER NINE New York, NY

be paying seemed to be high treason. But that inner light I was always in touch with was growing more faint and dim. I felt I had to get help or the low flame would be extinguished. I was close to walking dead. The ride on this bus was my surrender, facing internal voices of judgment. My body felt as if it would crack in two starting from the center of my heart. Restraining my inner thoughts was beginning to feel impossible. I wondered if I'd blow and begin to rant like some helpless beings I'd witnessed aimlessly walking the streets of New York.

The stop on East 92nd Street finally came. I arrived at the airtight brick office building entrance to find my way to the second floor where the therapist's suite was located. The silence was eerie as I waited in the anteroom. There was an odd ambient noise filtering through the area.

Gosh, I hope another patient won't enter, I thought to myself feeling my jaw clenching a little tighter. I didn't think I could handle a stranger's presence in this setting. I wondered what would be on the other side of the therapist's office door, and how I was going to maneuver, even though I was there of my own volition. Already, I was practicing how I would be a perfect patient. Obedient and responsive.

Finally, the door opened slowly. The bearded male therapist was soft-spoken and very tall with a receding hairline. He reminded me of a giant, gentle teddy bear. Ushering me in, he asked me to take a seat on the couch which threw me into fear. A couch, an office with a closed door, and a man brought on a clenched feeling in my stomach. I sat.

Softly, he asked, "Why did you make this appointment?"

After shifting uncomfortably, I said, "My life is out of control and completely unmanageable."

With sharp clarity, I began to explain I was stuck in an unhealthy relationship, repeating patterns echoing the dysfunction between my parents, and was losing morals.

Almost instantly, he began asking questions about how much I drank and if there was a history of alcoholism in my family. Silently, I wondered why he was asking questions about my drinking.

"My great-grandfather died of cirrhosis of the liver. And my dad drinks all the time," I answered. I didn't understand how alcohol use in my family or my own drinking could connect to the problems I was experiencing.

"I drink, too," I added nonchalantly.

The therapist asked me to stop drinking while I was in treatment and to check out Alcoholics Anonymous (AA). Though confused, I was willing. The pain inside and out, with anxiety that was almost indescribable, had me up against a wall. I would have stood on my head in the middle of Fifth Avenue if I were told it would help.

"Why should I go to AA meetings?" I asked.

Luckily this guy was savvy. He told me, "If you go to AA meetings you'll learn about your father's drinking problem."

He also suggested I attend Adult Children of Alcoholics (ACOA) to understand how living with an alcoholic father had affected me.

At this point, when someone of authority was trying to help me by giving me a suggestion, I generally followed their direction. In this case, it was a definite plus. To my credit, and fortune, off I went on my exploratory process, no more questions asked. I was so exhausted as well as phobic and falling away from my goals, I was ready to surrender.

My first AA meeting was mesmerizing. A young man with sandy straw-colored hair, preppy relaxed khakis, and a worn white button-down shirt stood up to get the meeting started. He seemed to exude such a sense of ease and comfort I was completely riveted. I wanted that sense of internal comfort he seemed to be easily transmitting.

The opening literature read aloud by various volunteers talked about humility, peace, and serenity. I realized I didn't know what serenity and peace were as they related to my life. I mostly knew drama and anxiety. Peace and serenity were not something I was consciously seeking though they sounded foreign and appealing.

After readings and an introduction, a middle-aged man spoke at the front of the room for a long while about his upbringing and experience while drinking. He talked about feeling desperate, depressed, alone, and out of control, bottoming out from alcoholism after driving his car through a Harrods department store window in London during a blackout. Of course, I thought, *I've never done that*, comparing specifics rather than emotions and feelings. I left the meeting relieved there was still drinking time left for me. I loved hearing the story and felt so curious and at home at the meeting, I continued to go for research. I found an AA meeting in my neighborhood, a few blocks from my apartment, and decided to stick to not drinking alcohol. It was scary, but for me, the support of a group of people refraining from alcohol gave me the strength to do the same. The fog started to lift.

The Adult Children of Alcoholics or ACOA meetings were riveting. The group was very small. There may have been seven of us gathering around a conference table hearing distant horns and sirens of the city half a dozen floors below. I couldn't believe the members were freely revealing stories of exactly what I had experienced as a child, describing emotions that fit me to a T – an impending sense of doom, danger lurking, and daily insecurity. I was indirectly trained not to let those secrets out, especially not to others. After several meetings, I began to speak too. Years of fear and anxiety fell out onto the table and began melting. I had decades to defrost.

One of the suggestions of both groups was to get phone numbers and

CHAPTER NINE New York, NY

call members between meetings. The suggestion terrified me. Making a call and connecting with someone else seemed frightening. I knew it could lead me out of isolation to a better state of health, so I started the process. I got a little book with an image of a punk rock baby complete with a mohawk and face paint in a diaper on the front screaming into a microphone. I taped a quarter in the back of the book in case I was out, had to make a call, and didn't have the correct change.

Many practical tools for living were being revealed. What I didn't realize was that I used these new tools as a weapon against myself. Growing up with unpredictable parenting, I developed a tendency to accept more blame than belonged to me along with shame and self-judgment. I was a confused ball of angry rage topped with guilt and submissiveness. These attributes collided and I was a sitting duck to predatorial pests. My self-hate was nothing short of a tsunami in proportions and while I was seeking a kind, loving parent, by habit, I was a magnet for those looking to suck me dry. Deep in my being, I knew I was full of a bright, inner-light but I wasn't sure how to navigate my way toward trusting and embracing it.

Sessions with my therapist were helping though I initially found the process frustrating. A big chunk of the work was in identifying my emotions. It was aggravating. I wanted the therapist to hand me a list and just give me a clue about what I was feeling. After years of shutting down, and stowing my emotions carefully away, it was difficult digging to discover basic feelings like happy, mad, sad, or glad. It was also a challenge to get to know my preferences, my humanity, and my esteem scoured back.

Newly sober, I was undergoing the delicate dance of identifying and detonating inner demons, when my boss tried to seduce me like many of his want-to-be-actress victims. He chased me around the office one afternoon and tried grabbing my crotch. Shocked, I hurriedly collected my stuff and got out the door, shaken yet trying to find calm and assimilate the attack.

Barbara Walters, the ABC anchor and host, was one of my personal training clients which I had taken up as a side business. It was a funny connection to be working directly with her after watching her on tv with admiration when I was growing up. She took one look at me before our session the next morning and knew something was up. I never usually shared my personal grief, but it came rolling up and out. After I confided in what was going on in my office, I sensed right away I touched a chord. She offered to come to work with me later that morning and confront my boss.

I wouldn't allow it.

I quit a day later. I collected my belongings and left on a Friday with no other job to go to and minimal savings. I went straight to the gym and realized in hindsight I'd forgotten some items that would have been helpful. I walked back to the office instead of heading home after my workout to discover the locks on the office door had been changed.

All of twenty-five, and newly sober, with barely three months of savings in the bank, I decided to open my own talent brokerage firm. I was living in a sunless studio apartment on the Upper West Side where you had to crouch down on the ground below the window and tilt your head up to see a sliver of the sky between the buildings to check the weather. I was praying I'd have enough guts to stay away from the abusive relationship I finally had pried myself away from as I went through this process. Money was a tool my ex-boyfriend used to manipulate and control me. I knew he'd rear his head as soon as he was bored or lonely and I hoped I was strong enough to stay away.

At Broadway Bazaar, I found a 3 x 3 black square desk for my white, one-line phone with a curly cord continually tangling and eventually a very large desktop computer. It didn't take long to realize clients weren't going to automatically appear, I'd have to take some action steps. After research, I purchased the *Standard Directory of Advertising Agencies,* which was a very big thick red book, and proceeded to cold call ad agencies one by one offering to match celebrities to their brands.

Making fifty cold calls a day, whether I liked it or not, pitching my capability of bringing talent to brands, I was praying I could land a deal. I was absolutely determined to make the fifty calls and would tally each one with a small mark in pen on a sheet of paper as if in doing so, magic would bring me what I hoped for, clients and cash.

I remember being exhausted and frightened in my little studio apartment, especially now that assuaging those feelings of fear with alcohol was out of the question. One evening I got down on my knees, bowed my forehead to the ground, and asked for help. I felt a warmth like someone was placing a blanket on me from my toes to just over my shoulders. It was profoundly soothing. I felt my fear immediately soften.

Donny Deutsch, who was running his dad's ad agency on Madison Avenue at the time, was referred to me and asked if I could deliver Andy Warhol for his client, the tri-state Pontiac dealers. I wasn't one to turn away work or challenges, so I agreed to try.

When I couldn't track down the number for the Factory, Andy's home, and business studio, I took the subway from my Upper West Side apartment down to East 33rd Street and knocked on the Factory door which was one in a long row of brownstones on the block. Fred Hughes, Andy's longtime business manager, answered looking at me quizzically through rimmed spectacles. I explained why I knocked.

Much to my relief and surprise, he said, "Come back tomorrow at this time and I'll let you speak with Andy."

I was elated, and sweating bullets. It felt like a lot was going to be riding

CHAPTER NINE New York, NY

on that conversation.

The very next day at the appointed hour I showed up and after a short wait, true to his word, Fred ushered me into Andy's studio. I was a little star-struck. There he was, Andy Warhol, live and in person, working intensely at a tall table under a pin spotlight with colored pencils. In one of my earliest celebrity meetings, I noticed the inventory I was taking of this demi God's humanness - his energy to me read, 'driven by fear' in flashing letters.

Fred shut the door leaving me alone with the modern art master and his three little dogs, pure-breed Pugs, who were running around the studio snorting. I took a deep breath. I was scared, really scared. Andy didn't look up or acknowledge me in any way. I knew this might be a tough sell, but I also knew Fred wouldn't grant me an audience with Andy unless he knew there was some chance.

"My name is Susan. I am working on behalf of an advertising campaign for the Tri-State Pontiac dealers," I nervously began to explain listening to my voice wobble and feeling my body getting hot.

I went on to explain he'd be appearing in an on-camera TV commercial. He seemed to have no interest in what I was saying, scribbling incessantly. His only pause was when one of his dogs would begin to gnaw at his pants leg. He'd stop, lean down, and like a proud papa, scoop the pooch right up, holding the fur baby close to his heart cooing.

Finally, he looked at me and in a very small and contained voice said, "Really, why should I do this?"

I stopped breathing and spontaneously words were almost said through me, "Because your Pugs can be in the shot with you!"

Of course, I really had no idea if that was true, but I felt I had nothing to lose at this point. He stared me down in complete silence for what seemed like forever, and then looked at his precious dogs in his arms, back at me, and said," I'll do it!"

And he did.

It was an amazing deal and one that would trademark my abilities to convince talent to do things they might not ordinarily consider. I felt a huge relief, yet little acknowledgement. I simply thought anyone would have this ability and skill set.

Just after the Gary Hart debacle when he dropped out as frontrunner of the Democratic race for president over extramarital affairs, Donna Rice – one of his paramours - agreed to my plea to endorse a young Neil Cole's No Excuses Jeans for another maverick ad agency owner, Richie Kirschenbaum of Kirschenbaum, and Bond. Soon after, I would deliver Geraldine Ferraro to do a spot for Diet Pepsi.

It was really fulfilling when I brought a deal to my former ICM Artist's boss who had packed the beaten-up brown cardboard box of my belongings and told me I was fired for interviewing for another job. Her client was the renowned cellist, Yo-Yo Ma and we were closing a deal with an energy company for Yo-Yo that was a win all the way around. It felt great!

In between making fifty cold calls a day, I'd go to an AA meeting on the Upper West Side of Manhattan. This kept me from picking up a drink. It also helped with social isolation. Slowly, very slowly, my fear of people began to soften. I started to connect with others. It was reassuring to be part of a 'club' so to speak and to be validated. Somehow, I felt more legitimate, whole, and like I authentically belonged. I was also gaining tools I'd never received on how to live minus a drink.

Though I was good at what I did and made a lot of money for talent and agency owners, I wasn't the best at asking for the money I deserved. My lack of self-worth and self-sabotaging traits would take me time to dissect and detonate.

My skills in attaching talent to brands eventually did lead me to television, though I had no experience or training in the area. I remember my boyfriend from college who had studied Radio and TV and graduated with a full-fledged degree, telling me I couldn't work in the field after I'd expressed an interest.

He assured me, "If you have no experience or professional training, it's not going to happen."

I thought that was silly. I never let those things stand in my way. I've never believed a piece of paper is necessary to get ahead in the job world or anywhere for that matter. My ability in attaching talent to projects was valued. It got me jobs as a talent booker with Vh-1, Hearst, and CNBC. Eventually, when I proved merit, I was placed straight into producing for television.

CHAPTER 10
SHIFTING GEOGRAPHY TO UNKNOWN TERRAIN

Once I stopped drinking, I needed a spiritual connection to stay grounded for a feeling of inner safety. Drinking had erroneously filled this emotional gap. I was carrying ancient anxiety and looking for something practical minus rules, shame, guilt, and blame.

Marianne Williamson's interpretation of *A Course in Miracles* was my vehicle. She was teaching practical human compassion, delivering fresh reality to my world. I would go to her electrifying lectures at a small church on Manhattan's upper west side. The magic was tangible. Marianne used to bunk at my friend Tara's apartment which was nearby. She moved at lightspeed and was turning heads, including Oprah's.

I remember being absolutely gobsmacked when she relayed the story of a very rude cab driver she experienced on her way into the city from the airport earlier in the day. Her answer to his rudeness was to tip him, double. It was her way of teaching us when people were angry, rude, and abrupt they were crying out for help, and love. We could be the answer to that call.

Her simple teaching made a practical dent in my armor and a deep shift in my consciousness. It helped thaw some of the steeped mentality ingrained in my belief system: 'eat or be eaten' and the stinginess of 'there's only so much to go around.' Slowly I began to look at my world and fellow humans differently.

There were many more concepts and beliefs I was living by in need of a new perspective. I was defensive, suspicious, and chock full of a deep-seated fear of being punished and judged. Feeling inadequate topped with fear of abandonment completed my inner terror of rejection.

Now I felt a low beam of light beginning to shine on my debilitating and programmed darkness. A tiny crack began to form in the concrete barricade I had built within and around me since early childhood, falsely protecting myself from deep trauma. This was a real chance to remove the barbed wire that enveloped me - all the barbs turned inward. It was a chance to break my isolation, connect, and begin to live more freely.

Going to 12 Step meetings and attending self-realization workshops, I could hear members share struggles with similar feelings and circumstances. I began to identify with their emotions rather than compare circumstances. Falling to all methods of escape, choosing to split from a true center and imploding were common traits. Negating personal values coupled with shame gave way to a malicious lack of self-understanding. Now I was able to recognize I was not alone in how I felt.

I believe I was born pure, with a plan and path for lessons I wanted to face in this life doing my best to fulfill the road map I came in with though directives were difficult. Through compassion, love, and kindness I began to experience bits of internal and external peace. Bravely embracing a way up, through, and out of destruction rather than projecting it outward became the new touchpoint for thriving. Receiving a small taste of inner freedom gave me hope and something to strive toward with a new outlook. Trusting enough to believe I could shift my past creating a new present began to seem possible.

My jobs were growing bigger with more pressure. I was ferreting my way alone figuring it out as I went along. By the time I was twenty-nine, a deal came in that seemed identical to the role I played with my parents. I was in the middle of two parties as a broker. Circumstances grew complicated quickly and kicked up historic fears and trauma. I sank into a clinical depression. I was working almost around the clock in an attempt to keep up and began to feel myself splitting out of my body. I was no match for the emotions this project was triggering. Pain mushroomed. I didn't know if I could hang on long enough to come back comfortably into my body. I felt as though I was watching a show from above, just as I had at points in childhood.

My friends realized the state I was in and decided to do an intervention. They suggested I check in to a hospital program in Florida for co-dependency and addiction treatment.

"I'll go," I muttered, tears rolling down my cheeks.

I couldn't feel the tears. Shifting my eyes downward and feeling shame I watched the tears with detachment. Realizing my disconnected state, one of my friends boarded the plane with me to Florida, delivered me to the hospital and flew right back. She saved my life. I couldn't have made the trip on my own. Though four years sober it was my first journey to experience rehab. This was a twenty-eight-day program for codependency. It was combined with those getting sober.

Not exactly where I thought I'd find myself after four years of recovery from addiction and spiritual seeking, I knew it was a gift to be in the tempo-

CHAPTER TEN Shifting Geography to Unknown Terrain

rary cocoon of the facility. I was numb with the veil of depressive darkness that draped me and felt as if I just screwed up my whole life. I couldn't stop obsessing about the deal I'd left behind and how it would all work out. The impulsive need to be in control was overwhelming.

Suicidal thoughts were raging with vengeance and I couldn't lower the volume. I was required to check in with the front desk four times a day to discuss my level of suicidal impulses.

"I didn't think of killing myself this morning," I mechanically reported to the nurse on duty in a flat monotone.

Wondering if the depression cloaking me would ever lift, I had some blood work done. When the results came in one of the recommendations was a medication to boost my serotonin levels, an antidepressant. Though popular at the time, I was very against pharmaceutical medication. I didn't understand that you could be sober and simultaneously on non-addictive medication. I fought the idea of taking it.

Finally, the staff nurse threatened me, "Either take the medication or the doctor will lock you in the psych ward attached to the hospital!"

My mother's words came flooding through her statement amplifying my fear and disorientation. "You'll end up in a psych ward! You're crazy!" the old continual messaging reverberated loudly in my mottled brain. It was my turn to decide.

That night, I quietly faced my mother's threats coming to life in that arid Florida institution. Here was my opportunity. Either go crazy as my mother projected or accept what was being prescribed as help. I didn't want to take medication, but I didn't want to end up in a psych ward either, fulfilling my mother's prophecy. On my knees at the side of my bed, I asked for help.

The next morning, a young and angelic seventeen-year-old recovering heroin addict with beautiful auburn ringlets stretching below her shoulders stopped me. She'd been in rehab multiple times trying to break loose of her addiction. We spoke a bit in the hallway. I brought up my fear of taking medication.

Sensibly, she asked, "If you weren't a recovering addict, went to a hospital with your symptoms, they did tests and suggested medication, would you take it?"

Explained that way, my decision seemed like a no-brainer. I was stunned at the wisdom of this young and delicate teen. Reluctantly, I took my pill at the appointed time later that morning.

I was shrouded in what felt like slate gray, unable to touch my viscosity, separate from myself in a new way. I was feeling lost like a lamb and wondering if there was a slaughter, hanging on for another choice. Death continued to seem a better idea than living.

Part of the hospital program was to walk to a nearby park for physical exercise and air. I had a strong connection to my physical body through all my years of dance and athletics. The depth of the depression made this seem elusive. The hot muggy stillness of the Florida summer day only seemed to replicate what I was projecting as hell. Bending forward to touch my toes seemed surreal as if my lower extremities belonged to someone else. Walking on the way back to the treatment center, almost without consciousness, I attempted to step into the path of an oncoming truck. A fellow patient noticed, grabbed my arm hard, and jerked me back. He said nothing, instead, he gave me a piercing look. A piece of me knew this wasn't the right choice and felt relief while a second portion of me felt defeat.

Eventually, days added up and therapy sessions began doing their job. Controlling what felt like an uncontrollable world, I was monitoring every bite of food I took in, swinging toward anorexia, dropping eighteen pounds while the depression was beginning to lift. After twenty-eight days, I was deemed fit to return to my former world. Relieved yet scared, I was feeling the same wafting fear and excitement I'd felt leaving my small town to work at the shore for the summer, going from the shore to a big college, going from a big college to a bigger city. I felt vulnerable. Going back to the constant and clanging din and frenetic pace of city life seemed daunting.

My boyfriend had taken care of my business project and informed me he'd be keeping the profits as payment for his services. Quickly, I was back to my former life with my recent experience lurking. Instead of seeing a therapist, I graduated to a psychiatrist. I felt intimidated. He seemed so monotone and sedate. The piped-in noise seeping through the ventilation system so patient privacy could be honored didn't help. Everything felt airless and contrived and I felt as if I had to defend myself to escape this setting instead of gaining self-understanding.

I stayed on the prescribed medication, deciding no matter what would come, I would not be willing to suffer deep depression again. Once experiencing a fall to the depths of bleakness depression created, I knew it, and it was familiar. I felt I had a decision and choice not to allow myself to plunge that deep with the tools and awareness I'd earned.

My ability in attaching talent to projects ultimately led to the world of television. It was an exciting format and where I'd wanted to head as a child growing up. Roger Ailes was running CNBC and had launched another network, *America's Talking*. Through a connection, I was summoned to headquarters over the bridge from New York City to Ft. Lee, NJ. My mission was to bring celebrity talent to the unknown talk channel. It was a difficult sell and celebrities weren't flocking.

Divine guidance intervened with the spontaneous idea of going to a red-carpet event, interviewing celebrities about the cause, and then asking them

CHAPTER TEN Shifting Geography to Unknown Terrain

to look straight to the camera and say, "My name is (celebrity) and you're watching *America's Talking*." I grabbed a cameraman and off we went.

The celebrity-infused promos weighed the network quickly. Major talent indirectly endorsing the network caught attention. My blast of creativity caused copycatting within other promotional divisions on cable channels. It also got me out of the promotions department into a coveted job as a producer of live programming.

My boss in promotions opened the door to his corner office and summoned me. He sat me down and said my work had caught the attention of CEO Roger Ailes who wanted to see me up in his office right away. I looked at him rather sheepishly as I didn't understand what the fuss was all about. I also felt a true sense of loyalty as this guy had really let me take the ball and run with it. My boss told me they wanted to move me out of promos and into producing for the network.

I didn't understand what a producer did or was but found it was exactly what I had done with the promos. Create the kernel of an idea, put the pieces together, and manifest the vision.

Up I went to see Mr. Ailes, who was kind and complimentary. I became unnerved when he asked his secretary to close his office door where he kept me for what seemed quite a while. He shared a bit about his beloved mother in Florida, which for some reason seemed odd in what I thought was a business meeting, and then began asking me a lot of personal questions about my family. "Are you close with your family? Do they live nearby? How often do you go home to visit?" asking the questions in quick succession as if he'd done this before and it was familiar.

This is a bit of an odd conversation, I thought quietly to myself. Dismissing my thoughts, the conversation concluded, I thanked him and left his office.

Several years later, my former boyfriend from college had left CNN and was working at Fox News Channel when then-Chair, Roger Ailes, was dismissed over sexual misconduct. We spoke. He was concerned Roger may have been inappropriate with me and suggested I read an interview in the *New Yorker* about the matter. Reading the piece, chills ran down my spine and my blood went cold. The interview Roger gave me on the day he summoned me to his office was the one described in the article; the exact one he'd given each of his victims. Thank goodness I didn't pass that test.

New York City was losing its magical luster. I spent weekends away in a secluded cabin on 120 acres in the Catskill Mountains where my soul felt a fleeting sense of harmony and peace. Weekdays were spent toiling in a chaotic, adrenaline-filled TV news bureau where I was shutting down emotions and feelings. Desensitization was becoming natural and seemed like a badge of honor as it had in my family. Every other word out of my mouth was not very polite and generally started with the letter 'f'. Part of me knew the newsroom was a perfect place to hide from the after effects of my childhood. If I stayed, I wondered if I'd become an automaton working in television news, further exploiting, and terrorizing that wounded little one tucked away deep inside of my heart.

I had a layer of plastic falsity around me knowing how and when to trot out people-pleasing remarks, make connections, and leap up and over toward my intended career goals. A piece of me was deadening. I was lost, anxious, and unsettled. I darted from place to place rather than indulge in breath or time and isolated as much as possible. It seemed easier. My schedule became rigid and controlled which helped me feel safe yet blocked real intimacy. I had difficulty making plans with friends and keeping them as any deviation from my schedule felt unsafe. The barricade around me was growing thicker and more fierce. I screamed for some type of help that I didn't know how to manifest.

A dear friend suggested a trip abroad to Spain, Morocco, and Portugal. I jumped at the opportunity. While in Morocco, we ran into a bit of trouble with our guide who assumed we would be buying expensive rugs to make up for the money he'd invested in giving us an inexpensive tour of the country by car. He began to threaten us. On the way back to Tangier from Marrakech, we ended up getting pulled over by police multiple times for his reckless speeding. I was terrified my friend and I would be hauled off to some prison, never to be seen or heard from again. Madly, I was rearranging the contents inside of my purse to try and control what felt like a chaotic and dangerous situation. My answer to feeling at risk, in danger, and out of control was to organize, clean, and try to make my outside surroundings perfect. I was replicating what I had done at home while growing up to stave off beatings.

Once we were back in Tangier, and the night before we were to board a ferry to return to Spain, our guide disappeared with our rental car. With no trustworthy official help, I spent the night worrying if my credit card would cover a stolen vehicle. At the last moment, our missing guide and car showed up. He begrudgingly took us back to the ferry station, following us through customs and onboard the ship. He found the nearest officer and began to plead his case,

"They're thieves. They stole my money!" he shouted.

The officer took our passports and questioned us but ended up returning our passports. Once we docked in Gibraltar, he was at it again with his accusations. Luckily, we escaped.

Another dear friend, who I had met on jury duty, called soon after I had returned to NY to invite me to Los Angeles. She was launching a nationally syndicated talk show and wanted me to bring talent to the table. I was ready for a change and said "yes," almost instantly, with little thought.

The next morning, I woke up with a lump in my throat and the same fear in my belly that I felt about going to New York as a college intern. Intuitively

CHAPTER TEN Shifting Geography to Unknown Terrain

I knew there was no turning back and it was time for me to make a change. Moving to LA for this job was my way out.

I threw myself a small goodbye party, packed my belongings, and off I went, a puddle of nerves and excitement. Intuitively I knew, this was the next necessary step for my soul to grow and I needed the sun Southern California promised.

New York had a grounding. You knew where you stood. People were often brutally honest. Geographically, we were all packed in tightly. LA felt like an unending sandbox that was continually going through a giant sifter; nebulous, amorphous, and shaky like the earthquakes that rumbled through town. You didn't know where you stood and while everyone seemed nice to your face, it was behind your back that seemed worrisome. The transient nature of the sunny land of golden honey is nefarious.

Initially, I couldn't get a feel for who would be a friend and who was a business associate. It seemed like a one-trick town, the entertainment industry, with lots of self-absorbed achievers clawing their way through the gutters wanting to meet people not for who they were at heart, but rather their connections and what they may do for you.

I was across the country from all I had known but was going to make the most of every opportunity. Part of the disorientation was that the ocean was on the wrong side. I simply could not get a hold of East and West. I'd never driven with four or five lanes of the road on one side of the barricade and four or more lanes on the other side. Off-ramps could come quickly as well as a chaotic merge. I owned a car in New York, but the traffic moved much more slowly with fewer lanes.

My jury duty friend, who would be my boss, generously allowed me to stay at her home with her partner, who welcomed me graciously. She was at Upfronts in New York where all the networks were trotting out their newest shows. Calling from New York, she insisted I go to a running treadmill class the following morning taught by a guy named Barry. Not wanting to miss a beat on my quest for fitness, off I went for the 6:30 am class. It was right up my alley… spinning for the treadmill. Barry was a love. A short, completely ripped doll who spoke in a very hoarse voice and rode around in a dented beat-up compact car of some type with his part Native American boyfriend named Chance.

Barry's class helped give me a feeling of home. Fitness has always been a strong connection for me and a source of self-esteem. Later, when Barry was leaving the studio where he worked to form his own business, I suggested he run a boot camp to lock in clients for a month of income. At least he'd know he could count on a month of memberships. *Barry's Bootcamp* was born and would become a global franchise.

I knew not to overstay my welcome with my friend and her partner after my experience in New York. I went straight into finding my guesthouse in the Hollywood Hills. I assured my east coast friends I would find it. A co-worker who was from Los Angeles just laughed when I told him of my plan. He kind of giggled and told me that guest houses for rent were difficult to find and wished me luck.

After a few false starts, during which I at least learned a little more about LA's sprawling geography, I found my guest house in a historical pocket across the street from the Hollywood Bowl. Not wanting to repeat wearing out a welcome like I had when I first moved to New York, within three days, I was out of my friend's home before she'd even returned.

It felt like a fresh start. It was different living in a newly remodeled "tiny house" amidst the Hollywood Hills and beautiful bougainvillea. It was bright and clean, with white tiles, light wood, and an oversized Jacuzzi bathtub. If I circled my hilly neighborhood, I could see the Hollywood sign as well as walk the terrain where Hollywood Golden Age stars Rudolph Valentino, Charlie Chaplin, and Bette Davis had once lived.

I got to know Los Angeles through my job, bringing celebrities to the table at a new TV talk show, and through fitness – running, swimming, biking, and yoga. At the tail end of living in New York, my focus went more strongly to triathlons having been a marathon runner. After suffering injuries running long distances, I thought I'd spread the training out to include swimming and biking to soften all of that running.

I was proud of myself for making the move while the loneliness of being single in a new city brought forward uncomfortable feelings of loss. Fear of abandonment set off a shock of jittery nerves through my central nervous system. I wasn't very good on my own. I didn't have trust in myself, which made absolutely no sense. There was a cavernous, blackened pit inside of my being I wasn't willing to acknowledge or address. Los Angeles was a very difficult place to be single and date. It seemed as soon as you'd show interest, bam, the chase was over, and the potential candidate was gone. It was a lot of fantasy and not much substance.

Luckily, one of my spin instructors from New York was in town visiting a friend. We were introduced and became like long-lost and beloved sisters almost immediately. We'd laugh and confide in each other with our angst and miseries and prop each other up time and again.

Along with triathlons, my meditation practice blossomed as did my study of yoga. I was becoming more interested in yogic texts, month-long silent retreats, and Ironman triathlons. I was starting to revel in California life when I stumbled upon an individual who would become one of the biggest heart-cracking lessons and teachers of my life.

I'd been single for the longest period ever, maybe a little over a year, which should tell you something. I was always seeking a significant other. I think

CHAPTER TEN Shifting Geography to Unknown Terrain

it started with Billy Fritz in second grade. I never felt whole unless I was involved in a relationship. Somehow, I had a faulty belief I'd be destitute, arrested, and put in prison without a steady boyfriend or partner. I thought I needed a relationship to prove I was worthy. It felt ancient and deep, to a cellular level. I had a dent, no I had a crater, blown through my confidence seemingly filled only by a man. Though I'd come a long way, I had never fully healed from the initial wounding of my grandfather, father, and oldest brother. Claiming my personal space as my own, impenetrable by perpetrators, and feeling entitled to boundaries was off-limits.

The false belief, that I was incomplete without a man, proved dangerous. Shoved down so deep in my psyche, there was no way I was going to dive in after it. I was enslaved to the thinking I needed allegiance to a male partner to be 'safe.' It would be another decade and a half before I could even begin to puncture that hellish belief.

TOXIC FAMILY

CHAPTER 11
THE FAÇADE OF LOVE

My birthday party was at Bar Marmont on the compound of the famous Chateau Marmont in West Hollywood. I was the new girl in town and the invite list included mostly friends from work and friends of theirs along with my new friend Melissa. She was dating a guy who showed up with another couple of guys in tow.

One of them kept asking if he could buy me a drink, which I kept refusing. I didn't drink. He was tall with a cowboy embroidered shirt and beaten-up leather jacket with motorcycle boots beneath his washed-out baggy jeans. For some reason, he reminded me of a golden retriever. His shoulder-length hair was swinging side to side as he spoke. On his third ask, I surrendered. I accepted sparkling water. There was something admirable about him continuing forward after repeated rejection. My dad had always said if a guy asked me to dance or asked me out, I had to say yes, once. We spoke a bit and exchanged cards.

I'd flown my mom out to watch her 'grand' dog for ten days while I would be away on my very first week-long silent meditation retreat. After the party on the way home in the car, she was going through the business cards.

She pulled out the one from the sparkling water guy and commented on his last name saying with enthusiasm, "Oh, Susan, this one is Hungarian, did I meet him?"

I didn't know it when we spoke, but he was Hungarian with the last name of Bartok. My family on my mother's side was very proud of their Hungarian heritage. The attention he showered on me appealed.

I left for the meditation retreat anxious, not knowing if I could make it for a week making no eye contact and remaining silent. It seemed rude not speaking with dozens of other meditators at a lovely little retreat center in Encino, CA.

I remember watching as the other participants unloaded their vehicles carrying zafus and zabutons (fancy meditation cushions) while I grabbed my oversized pillows and blankets. Cars ranged from beat-up Toyotas to flashy BMWs and a lot of Birkenstocks, the faint smell of Dr. Bronner's castile soap and garlic swirling in the air surrounding them.

After a brief introduction by the esteemed meditation teacher who led the retreat, Shinzen Young, we were formally sent into silence. His first Dharma talk, or main lecture, began. I kept looking around the room guessing at the personalities of the others. It was interesting to watch my internal judgments roll on and on. After four hours of sitting on the floor, we were excused to our rooms until pre-dawn the next day when the meditation bell called us to the first sit.

My brain was noisy. I wasn't used to keeping silent and not making small talk with a new community of people. It was uncomfortable and awkward. I had to use my training as a triathlete and practitioner of yoga to hold my focus.

The ringing and gongs of the meditation bell quickly became ingrained. I'd wait for that soft ding to signal the release and an all-clear from sitting in silence for thirty minutes – or sixty - and sigh when the bell would call us to return. We did lots of walking meditation, which involved very slow, methodical, small steps – not my usual 10K around a park. Perhaps most difficult was the eating meditation where each morsel of food was to be taken with full consciousness, utensil resting on my plate after each bite. A very tall stately gentleman with a buzz cut and longtime meditator led that process. It was excruciating.

"Look at your fork, pick it up and feel it between your fingers, feel the anticipation it may evoke. Look at your plate, what bite will you select?" His suggestions continued for what seemed an eternity.

My discomfort was climbing. I wanted to slip away as he was softly smiling with compassion.

Loneliness, comparisons, and judgments were stabbing through my thought process. Emotions still weren't my strong suit, they were in a constant stream. There was little to do but notice them. At the time, I didn't see identifying my emotions and thoughts as welcome navigation potentially leading to nirvana. I quickly marked and shoved them aside. All the intent and internal focus led me to a massive migraine headache. I felt homesick and wanted distractions. I had no idea a weeklong silent meditation retreat would be grueling.

Why did I do this to myself? I could have gone up the coast for a week at the beach instead of this, I thought quietly. Determined, I continued onward. I didn't want to be a dropout.

We were working up to the Yaza, an all-night period of meditation, or sits, which seemed to be a meditator's version of a marathon. I felt competitive about it like most things, yet wasn't sure I'd be able to make it through the whole night of sits. Being woken up in the middle of the night to my parents arguing put an indelible stamp on my anxiousness about sleep. I feared the night hours. Often, I'd go to sleep subconsciously afraid I wouldn't get enough rest.

I never got off east coast time since moving to California. I'd usually be up by 5 am to train in the swimming pool, run, practice Ashtanga yoga or drive to the other side of town and ride with a fierce road cycling pack. To keep my mind occupied and away from more raw emotion, I started fantasizing about another meditator. I decided he was the cutest in the circle and projected dreamy thoughts his way.

The Yaza came and I made it through, cementing my position of belonging in this meditating club. I transferred my competitiveness into meditation. After another day and a half, it all wrapped up with a triumphant talking circle to break the silence. It felt odd to be speaking after not speaking for so many days. And that male meditator I occupied myself with…as soon as he opened his mouth, I knew he was not for me, not at all. It gave me a strong insight into how my mental projections work.

After packing my belongings back into my car and saying goodbyes, I stopped at a nearby supermarket. My senses were heightened after a week of silence and holding focus. When checking out, I could literally hear the internal thoughts of the checker, just like I had when I was a child. It scared me and I shut it off quickly. Getting back to my guesthouse, I found my treasured Bernese Mountain Dog made it through a week with my mom and his dog nanny caring for him. I felt transformed with a new sense of focused clarity.

The Hungarian sparkling water boy called while I was away. I returned his call and we decided to meet for dinner. It turned out he worked a few blocks from where I was living. Rather than go together, I told him I'd meet him at the restaurant, my control kicking in. He turned out to be from my home state and we both had lived in New York City. We had some people in common as well as the type of work we did. He worked with a film retrospective non-profit, and I was working with American Movie Classics producing backstories on the golden age of Hollywood Films.

I was hesitant to get together with him again. Something didn't feel right. My friend Melissa met him at a party separately and encouraged me.

"You should hear how he talks about his mother," she said.

Melissa was taken by the adoration he obviously had for his mom, who was an artist welding metal sculptures in suburban Pittsburgh and appearing in B-rated Yakuza-themed movies in Japan pre-children. It was odd but I didn't have an understanding of why it mattered that a male had a love for their mom. Easily influenced and like a puppy, I discounted my intuition and followed Melissa's advice.

It was not long after our initial dinner that I realized he'd make a great on-camera expert, and I hired him for a shoot I was producing for AMC. His knowledge was intoxicating. He was brilliantly studied and great on-camera, composed and comfortable.

During the first sit-down interview for the network, I fell for him, hook, line, and sinker. It was as if a frying pan had fallen from the rafters banging me on the head and waking me up to his charms. I loved how he'd stand slouching into his hips like an actor at the bar posing. He was right out of one of the golden age films we'd discuss.

This might have been a clue...what I didn't realize was he really was posing and had spent a lifetime living through images from films he'd watched. Like me, he'd grown up in a very violent and chaotic home. He'd escape through movies as his tool for coping. And he had never taken the opportunity for internal work or deep self-reflection. He was gapingly wounded and completely untreated which was probably a subconscious piece of the attraction for me.

For now, he seemed dreamy. He said all the right things, love-bombed me to bits, and I fell hard for it all. I really thought I'd finally met THE one.

And I did.

It just wasn't THAT one. It was the one that would teach me one of the biggest lessons I believe I came here to learn, the depth of my power.

We had a lengthy courtship; I was wondering when we'd move in together. He created the perfect picture of what I thought I wanted. Respectful, adoring, funny, bright, articulate, and not the type to slip away from my grasp for better pastures. My abandonment fears consistently hamstrung me to picking from the lowest-hanging fruit.

Ultimately, I think the move-in time came so he could get help covering half of his rent. He'd sold a big movie script and was poised to sell another but that never did manifest. The script he sold went into turn-around, and unless it

CHAPTER ELEVEN The Façade of Love

went into production, the deal was done triggering monies barely equal to the hard costs. His non-profit job, though prestigious, hardly covered his existing bills.

There were additional red flags, mostly of entitlement, but I refused to entertain them. I was too busy pulling more than my share of the weight and distracted by his hypnotic compliments and acceptance of my quirks. Eventually, we married and ultimately had our beloved son.

We were living in a cramped, rat-infested bungalow in what had become a very trendy LA neighborhood. Opportunities seemed less abundant and pressures to be successful, especially as a new parent began compounding. He began to rely on me like a panicking drowning victim with their rescuer. I gave from a dark place emitting a deafening fear of abandonment. The terror of feeling deeply unworthy trenched me to eternity in the pit of my belly. My nervous system, running on empty over-responding at every hair-triggering turn.

I was completely blindsided by the unevenness of the relationship. He had the second bedroom as his functioning office, while I rented an office outside of the home, bearing all costs. His car was always parked in the one-car driveway, while I purchased and brought in all the groceries and diapers from available street parking. He reaped the rewards of our nanny, and I paid for her services. All simple metaphors for the imbalance in the relationship. I kept pointing three fingers back at myself whenever I'd point one at him thinking I had to be more generous, less spiteful, and stingy.

My world began getting smaller. I had trouble breaking a rigid routine. My need to compulsively clean was intensifying. I could not leave the house if something was out of place. My exercise schedule had to be adhered to as if my life depended on it and started way before dawn. I was looking, no pleading, for safety in these things.

I was also obsessed with buying a home. I never bought one when I was single. It didn't even cross my mind. I had a buried, bizarre belief that a single woman shouldn't buy her own home. I could draw a line directly back to the trauma of my parent's divorce and my mother assuring us that no man + house = big trouble.

Property values in Los Angeles were spiraling out of control and I was almost going mad walking the dogs in the pre-dawn light muttering under my breath, "I could have bought that house for $175k, or that one for $250K!"

Baseline price tags were now reaching three-quarters of a million and up.

After years of looking, I finally cobbled a deal together on a small San Fernando Valley bungalow. Going to the bank to wire the deposit, I was quaking writing down the numbers to be transferred. It was one of the few times my husband went with me on an errand. He seemed so nonchalant and expectant as if this happened every day. Of course, it wasn't coming out of his individual earnings. Later, I found out, to my horror, that those earnings weren't considered my own. We were married and in California, half was his regardless of his contributions.

On the way in the car to the closing, I was informed by the escrow officer that I had to come up with another $3,000 on the spot. Our debt-to-income ratio was too high. I didn't have debt. I didn't understand what the escrow officer was talking about. What I didn't know was that my husband had tens of thousands of debt on his credit card. His debt was my debt. Enraged, I came up with the cash and we closed the deal. The taste in my mouth was bitter. A joyous occasion felt dampened even though my husband promised he'd pay me back on his half of the house down payment.

The giant red flag over the down payment and extra unexpected cash I needed to come up with troubled me. I resented it. It also woke me up to money and marriage. Although I was proud of myself, the transaction felt lopsided. Rather than talk about it directly, it seeped out in venomous and castrating remarks. I took on the bulk of the expenses and repairs in our new home. The plumbing, electrical, flooring, and painting costs quickly added up. As each contractor came through, he'd address his comments solely to my husband and seething, I finally suggested to one that he look my way.

Towing the load, silently scornful was my normal way of operating. It felt safer to treat men as if they were incapable of taking care of me, in any way, to save disappointment and block intimacy. I was prepared to have men fall off balance, with no recourse but to save them. I'd be hyper-ready to pick up the pieces quickly, with efficiency, and with little complaint. I had survived that way. It was a taxing and faulty belief system beginning to show rot around the edges.

I was hard-pressed to defy my lack of belief in men. I had quite an ability to manifest and little radar to attract an equal partner. I don't think I wanted an equal partner. It may have proved too intimidating. My need to be in control and foist off feelings of abandonment or rejection had to reign supreme for me to feel safe. I knew it subconsciously but had no idea how to work with those beliefs to shift them. I was terrified of being without a man, so I compromised my own well-being in most relationships. As a result, I pulled way more than my fair share of the weight. Though deeply asleep to the patterning, I was beginning to awaken, with the not-so-subtle rath of an infuriated Grizzly bear.

My father's words to me when I was a teen echoed in my ears, "no one will want you unless you pay. Your tastes are too expensive, and you want too much."

My antidote was to silence my needs and desires, do the housework, buy the groceries, take care of our child, pay for childcare, and earn enough to pay the lion's share of the bills. I didn't feel entitled to ask for help from my hus-

CHAPTER ELEVEN The Façade of Love

band until it was too late. I silenced myself, afraid I'd be punished or abandoned if I brought up fair and just terms. I wanted him to magically realize the error of his ways. What I didn't understand was my partner wasn't capable of integrity or acting as an equal. He viewed me as an object to serve his needs and his self-absorbed tendencies blocked his ability to be responsible. I'd married a big piece of my father.

With a child and home to be responsible for, pressures began to mount. It was crushing, and I was being crushed. I remember leaving for a night job I had picked up to meet our monthly expenses, my husband was smiling and waving with our son from the front porch as I backed out of the driveway. He did not have a clue. He thought if he just posed, whistled, and sang enough happy songs all would be well… and he could continue to push me, the work mule, forward through the trough with a few adoring phrases. He could, he did, but the mirror of a fraudulent foundation was beginning to crack.

A master of manipulation, it turned out that there was truly no room for adult communication. My words would ricochet gaslighting me until I couldn't see clearly. I was beginning to melt. I couldn't put my finger on what wasn't working and more importantly, why I couldn't fix it. Worse, I was too dependent on the relationship.

What I did to appease the pain was to do what I'd always done, over-exercise and achieve athletically, using my own body as a tool to assuage pain and anesthetize myself in brutally punishing ways. I was training with a nationally ranked swim team before dawn, throwing Kettlebells later in the morning, and slipping into hot yoga along with walking the dog three times a day. Property taxes were coming due, and I was hustling my own work project. In combat mode, I maneuvered like a human machine. The machine was beginning to clunk and hiss.

And my bow began to break.

No matter how I would manipulate, chide, and perform, it wouldn't change my husband. And I couldn't stand up directly for myself. Not wanting my marriage to disintegrate, I got the idea of trying to make it all okay via paper. After doing some research, I felt a postnuptial agreement might legally even things out, protect my assets, and do the trick to save our marriage. I didn't want my family to break apart even though I knew our relationship was long past its due point.

We began mediation. After weeks, we ultimately got to the last point of contention.

I thought we were coming to an agreement and our marriage would be saved when my husband crossed his arms over his chest and with arrogance, belligerently looked at me with a piercing cold blank stare and said, "I'm hiring an attorney and filing for divorce."

The room went still.

Filled with fear, I knew in that instant this was the Universe doing for me what I could not do for myself. A small clear voice from the heavens whispered those exact words right into my heart. As I sat frozen at the conference table, time seemingly suspended, I noticed weight lifting from my torso; strength and peace seeping into the void. We both left the negotiating table quietly, got into separate cars, and returned to our shared home.

And then the real hell ensued.

My husband wouldn't leave the master bedroom, let alone the house. I met with the attorney I was referred to for representation the next day.

He sternly said, "Move out of the master and into another room as soon as possible. It's bad for your son otherwise."

I went home, and realizing my husband and son were out, immediately marched into the master bedroom, grabbed a corner of the heavy Queen-sized mattress, and began tugging, lifting, shoving, and sliding the heavy pad across the house, downstairs, into the den and through a door leading into the garage. Sitting on that mattress, on the cement floor, in a partially converted garage of the home I purchased, maintained, and improved woke me up to hard truths. Stunned, I was finally addressing the changes I needed to face. Our relationship was past its expiration date and my insistence to care for the behavior of another at my own expense to shelter the fears of abandonment had to shift.

I befriended a black widow spider that loved the metal door of entry and pretended not to hear the rustle of the rats that loved hiding under the dryer. This was the billboard I needed to fall on my head to wake me up completely from a deep sleep. I had to be crushed and cracked open on a new level. Another violent initiation was necessary to receive a masterful lesson about my power.

Spending over a year in this living circumstance, I chose to see that room in the garage as my monastery. With purpose, I transformed those four small walls into a protective womb, and a nest for personal digging, and re-purposing of obsolete beliefs. Everything I had learned and experienced came into play for me to navigate through this major life lesson I was facing. I noticed it and held on to the belief that I was prepared and able to take on this horror.

Week-long silent meditation retreats helped me hold a brutal no-contact. No contact meant no words and no engagement - even in the same living quarters with a man I had loved and lived with for fifteen years. It was shocking and necessary. It took tremendous discipline and restraint of natural impulses not to fight back. I was beginning to learn how strong I was as friends had always echoed.

Long marathons and triathlon training helped me maintain a fierce

CHAPTER ELEVEN The Façade of Love

focus and grueling tenacity. I knew my well-being was buoyed by the experience of endurance training which helped me through the arduous course of divorcing one I experienced as a narcissist.

Our nine-year-old son was amongst this which was dreadful. My concern was keeping him relatively content and safe in quite an insane situation. Every Saturday I would find a new activity for us to do together or with friends. Car museums, water parks, wild animal sanctuaries, beach days, climbing gyms, and obstacle courses gave us something to bond over and new experiences to file away as pleasant memories.

I was perplexed by the word narcissist as I now was defining my husband. I'd heard that word before, but it never made much impact. It was the same as hearing the word alcoholic, it never frightened me away. I didn't understand the mental, physical, and emotional dangers involved.

Googling narcissist led me to a plethora of information and an effective program I put into play that would keep me on the planet in the unraveling of my marriage. An endless loop of talk therapy didn't seem to be an answer. I found instead the Narcissistic Abuse Recovery Program or NARP effective. I was releasing trauma on a cellular level, letting go of belief systems and energetic patterning that created damaging behaviors. Retraining neural pathways was not optional. Pieces were coming together. It was making sense why I felt I needed a man to be safe and why I felt I had to bow down to a male master to feel whole. Through the NARP program, I also learned the template for divorcing a narcissist. No contact.

I was living under bizarre circumstances, changing the rules of engagement by holding no contact, and witnessing his mask fall to the ground, replaced by a macabre version of Medusa. The lie of it all was coming to light.

Actually, the recommended treatment for dealing with a narcissist is no contact and no verbal engagement. Written correspondence is repetitive and short. Though challenging in any circumstance, I went after the methodology as if training for an endurance race. Surrounding myself with loving friends and family members, I submerged into an abyss.

The experience touched every core wound - abandonment, betrayal, rejection, separation, loss, and broken trust. The fear was often close to overwhelming. Breaking an addiction to men by ferreting my way through this morass was my greatest challenge. The most frightening material aspect was wondering if I would be able to keep my son and myself in the home we so dearly loved. The home I purchased was like my World Cup. There was no way I wanted to stand by and allow my ex-to-be to swindle it away from not just me, but our son who loved his school and his home.

A brutal experience, my spouse did everything he could to wrestle our home away. When I was in disbelief by his lack of integrity and disregard for his son's future for the benefit of his own belly, I broke yet more denial over who I had married and the nature of my own disorder staying in the relationship with little regard for my well-being or that of our son. It helped me to stand up, though it was excruciating

At the time, I was convinced if I made it through this experience, I could make it through anything. It was a challenging transition filled with intense anxiety and an avalanche of old fears and terrifying bodily memories that came raining down.

At the time, I was studying the Law of Attraction as it seemed to be interpreted by experts. If I had a negative thought over the divorce outcome, I'd be frozen with fear, feeling there was no room for that energy to be emitted. I marched through the process mostly stoic, like a decorated Green Beret muttering positive mantras forcefully shifting my beliefs. Exhausted, the fear in my stomach of how I was going to pay attorney fees, what my home may appraise for, and how I was going to be able to keep it had my central nervous system working overtime. Trying to control the uncontrollable was impossible. Surrendering was the only option.

Each month the bills from the attorney were in the multiple thousands of dollars. My blood went cold if I opened an email in the middle of the night when sleep wasn't coming to see a new invoice. During this period, I was given a gift of insight realizing money could be a bit like Monopoly money. The numbers were big, yet each month I had what I needed. Though the fear was there, I couldn't deny I was being taken care of by what seemed a magical force.

Ultimately, I realized material things, like my home, were unimportant compared to the safety and sanity of my son and myself. Toward the very tail end of this experience, tensions began to mount as my husband became more desperate. I was ready to leave the keys on a table and walk away with my son and the clothes on our backs.

I knew I had to keep an eye out for the miracles. And that's exactly what I did. The first came in the form of one of the largest deals I'd ever made regarding financial return. I felt my angels had my back. I was stunned and grateful. The other was that I had loyal support from close friends and my family.

My ex-husband-to-be had done the typical action of almost every narcissist. He went on a smear campaign to friends and family, making me out to be a deranged kook who had suddenly gone off the deep end. He had been working on my dear aunt and uncle who were the only relatives I had on the West coast prior to the divorce. I witnessed his manipulation. They sided hard with him. It was painful to have family members turn against me, but I knew exactly what my husband was doing. Ultimately, my truth was what mattered. I had to be strong, not bite the bait, nor engage by reacting. I truly learned the restraint of pen and tongue.

CHAPTER ELEVEN The Façade of Love

When it got down to the nitty-gritty of the divorce settlement, suicidal depression began to rear its ugly head. Having experience, I knew its signs and signals. Rather than succumbing to the insidious whispers of depression, I asked seven friends to stand by on a certain day each week and committed to calling the one assigned for the day to check-in. If the friend didn't answer, and I was in trouble with suicidal thoughts, I'd commit in a message to call the next person on the list. This system literally brought me through the tail end of the trauma.

Ultimately, it was the six-figure check I wrote to settle the divorce agreement that got my husband to move out of the master suite and right onto his next victim. Narcissists disregard and discard only to pick back up again with their next source of supply while simultaneously trying to keep you on their hook. In a little over a year, he'd married again.

My cousin, the daughter of the uncle my ex turned against me, who provided support in my process, ended up in a similar situation experiencing her own divorce.

My uncle suggested she call me saying, "Whatever Susan did, worked."

Though my uncle attempted to be in touch, I learned enough to know not to make attempts to mend the relationship while wishing him well with silent mental messaging. He was triangulating, relaying information to my ex. Drawing a boundary and not taking care of my uncle's needs was new behavior for me. Breaking familiar co-dependant actions threatened my faulty sense of security yet eventually, clarity ruled. It proved to be the right decision.

Finally, there was a moment to sob. I barely allowed tears to escape during this whole process. With rivers of sadness inside, I didn't want to open floodgates. I felt I had to be strong for my son, and wiped away tears quickly, my body suffering from this faulty belief.

Working in the NARP program, co-parenting was less difficult than it might normally be. Holding a strict policy of 'no contact', in this case, modified contact in writing only, I had a solution that worked. With limited responses to zany, long-winded, bullying emails trying to lure me back into a web of illness my ex's power over me continued to slip away. His new wife was a Godsend. She treated my son with grace and kindness and that is where I needed to hold focus.

It was time for me to surrender self-inflicted punishment, own self-love, and discover who that battered, bruised, neglected, and muddied sweet child was inside me. Looking at my experience through a completely different lens, I see I welcomed my husband as a willing participant in my dysfunctional dance. I consider it one of the most masterful lessons of expansion this life has delivered to help reflect my authentic power. My inner rigid superhero was softening, slowly, melting drip by drop.

Here I was, in six-figure debt, a single parent, and a self-employed solo homeowner in Southern California. It was like the feeling after graduating college and being on my own for the first time, liberating with a twist of terror, now multiplied by eight.

My friends had always thought of me as strong and told me as much. Mostly, I felt it was a stoic front. Now I was entering an internal journey to find authentic inner strength and self-love not reliant on another for what seemed to be the first time in my life.

Though astonishing, I was able to practically remodel my entire home including the addition of a small guest suite to help with my mortgage, taxes, and insurance. Instead of a garage that was packed floor to ceiling with vinyl records, posters, DVDs, and vintage objects from my ex-husband, I was now earning income.

Absolutely terrified while nudging myself forward, I put one foot in front of the other facing fear. Wildly, everything kept falling into place. True to the words whispered to me at the end of mediation, the Universe had done for me what I could not do for myself. Breaking my pattern of addiction toward self-use and abuse and releasing me from the bondage of yet another predator I loved.

Now my work was to free myself from the predator I had cemented within my own system.

CHAPTER 12
CONTROLLING FATE WITH FORCE

Embroidering magical thinking into the fabric of my being was a false way to help me feel in control and safe. Guilt, as if I had done something against the law, perpetuated a feeling of being unworthy having had the divorce experience I did. There was an internal sinister and wafting fear continually whispering, "You're not safe without a man." I was certain I'd be damned and punished for escaping the silent and confusing hell of my marriage.

My money fears rode high. I had a six-figure debt to repay, a home to maintain, and a son to raise on my own. I wrote down every debt repayment I made toward eroding the huge mound with a golden marker on small slips of notepaper. I kept those paper slips in a tribute card I had made to my Bernese Mt. Dog once he died with his great face on the cover. After each payment amount and date, I'd write an affirmation like, "money is manifesting easily" and "debt is quickly being erased." I was determined to acknowledge my accomplishments.

A visitation directed me to shift my thinking and continual berating. In a dream my ex and the uncle he'd turned against me were together. When I saw them, a huge sense of shame washed over me for being bad and wrong. Disturbed, I awakened. Sitting up in my bed, I noticed a white and golden flecked misty and wet energy in my room. Telepathically, the gentle force was directing me to release any shame or guilt, urging me to self-forgiveness and affirming my ex and uncle as playing old and dying patriarchal masculine roles. The experience was profound. The energy was similar to the one when I was newly sober, on my knees with fear and blanketed by a soothing presence. Even so, it was still hard for me to convince myself I translated the message correctly allowing my guilt to drop through its gentle nurturing.

My days stayed mostly the same. A punishing and grueling physical exercise regimen; a need for the house to be immaculate; and attempts to be in control when I wasn't even close. Often equating my thoughts with what was manifesting and blaming myself when things went awry for not projecting positively, my narrow interpretation of the Law of Attraction was beginning to wear me down. I needed to find a better way.

Enraged with a limited lack of willingness to dive into the pool of seething red anger and wade through it, I felt shattered inside, mostly numb, and functioning on automatic at a frenetic pace. I didn't know who I was now with my self-identity changing again but knew this was a better path than where I'd been walking. It was the first time I heeded my gut remaining unpartnered. I had done so much inner and external work to survive the divorce, but now I was on the other side, feeling depleted. I was determined not to fall into my old behavior of co-dependent partnering.

Taking on massive construction projects in my home with minimal experience as my own contractor was more than a little stressful. It wasn't surprising, I was always challenging myself. The continual barrage of internal lambasting wasn't helping. There was good news as I was beginning to recognize the voice of self-hate when it was coming up. I had never selected materials for re-designing my home or learned steps for making over bathrooms or bedrooms, let alone converting my garage into a guest suite. Shaming myself instead of cheering myself on didn't make a lot of sense. The controlling judging old male and guilt-mongering old female loop of programming were at decibel ten.

My brother-in-law and sister invited my son and me to spend a few days with them at a compound in Mexico. When we arrived, I realized how empty and fragile I felt. We both seemed shell-shocked and though I was grateful to be there and for their more than generous invitation, it was hard to unwind.

This was a lot to take on alone, yet my old pattern to find a man, seek solace and some type of false protection was finally done. I couldn't imagine connecting in partnership. I didn't trust myself. Finally, I saw clearly when I was in a relationship, I usually insisted on dragging some male figure double my weight along for the ride while resenting it.

The words of my father were echoing, "Your tastes are too expensive… no one will want you."

Getting through the divorce and seeing my part in the set up though humbling, was revealing.

I was now in a place where I wanted to break embedded patterns based on fear of rejection and abandonment. Finding lasting self-respect within and

CHAPTER TWELVE Controlling Fate with Force

without was my new focus. For the first time, I didn't see a need to add a partner to my plan, and I was comfortable with the new equation.

I wondered if I would ever be able to let go, trust myself and allow a potential companion to get close enough to authentically partner with me. I thought of my maternal and paternal grandmothers, who confided when I had asked, that they would never again marry my grandfathers if given a choice. As much as I related to their journeys, I wanted a definite barricade to keep me safe from that fault line, secretly wondering if I might break the patterning.

Smashing an ancient faulty belief, and ending the need for a partner to be safe and whole seemed a rite of passage as if clearing ancient family lineage. Experiencing being okay and even happy solo, though new, seemed possible. Not with vengeance, but with the objective to truly come to recognize and appreciate my capabilities and build self-compassion was invigorating.

Firmly, I believe the journey through my marriage and divorce was to reflect a broken belief in knowing and trusting my own power. What did not make conscious sense was why I was deeply rooted in fear of surviving while I had been carrying most of the ball consistently in my relationships. It was odd, I had this rumbling inner panic of not being able to *make it* — ready to go under like I had in that lake when my father was first teaching me to swim. Looking further, it would be painful for me to truly rely on a partner. My fear of abandonment and experience of it was too great.

Another question that plagued me was how I would be able to release resentment that boiled within me over what I saw as a very unfair situation. Divorce stripped me of earnings and assets I clearly accumulated and left me in six-figure debt. It seemed unjust. To survive the aftermath of the divorce, I had to stop making my ex accountable in *any* way and begin to put the pieces together leading to a new way of living for me. This was the medicine I needed to create a different future. Hanging on to the resentment would not serve me. It was like eating rat poison myself and expecting my ex to suffer the consequences. Transforming my own thinking was the antidote.

Ultimately, I came to understand all the expenditures to my ex-husband were a grand lesson in generosity. Turning this experience on its head, on its side, upside down, shaking it, and looking at it from a new perspective with the help of profoundly gifted angelic healers was the ultimate answer to freedom.

Seeing it all as a necessary lesson to propel me to a better place was hard, and at times seemingly impossible. It reminded me of getting sober. I decided to trust the group, keep my head down, and not pick up a drink no matter what. Now, I had to put aside my resentment and make forgiveness my sole focal point or fall. It took discipline. I had to trust I was moving toward a very different mindset and way of living than I'd ever experienced. Trust was not my middle name; I did what I could.

I sent forgiveness to my ex when I'd catch myself boiling in wrath knowing it would serve me. It wasn't authentic. I was behaving like a little girl trying to be good for Santa Claus to deliver the approval of a Divine source and then be rewarded as a result. It was another outdated belief system needing shifting.

An accumulation of days helped wash away some of the pain. Friends helped. Remodeling my home helped. I saw the physical transformation and it was amazing. Putting the focus on caring for myself, my son, and our dog helped. Noticing little miracles like feeling a bit safer in my own body, compulsively cleaning less, and my work life improving all helped. I could sense the true gift of being released from the old paradigm of relationships taking on more meaning with each year as time passed.

Continuing to applaud myself with each payment I made toward the debt, I noticed I was now kinder to myself, and these moments were new wins. I'd recognize the horrendous beast of my inner self-talk rearing its ugly head to bat me down about how I could have been so conned, so blind, so manipulated, and manipulative. I found a way to quietly encourage a more soothing voice forward appreciating all I had done right. I also began embracing hard truth; I set this dynamic and scenario up to teach myself who I truly was, a powerfully capable, and loving human being.

CHAPTER TWELVE Controlling Fate with Force

Up to this point, there was a tremendous amount of anger, resistance, and hate I was taking on internally and gobbling up mistakenly in my relationships, in the workplace, and in friendships. When I took a further glimpse backward, I clearly saw this starting early in my childhood. Though familiar, I had to find a way to redirect this deeply empathic pattern.

Still trying to control my Universe through exercise, and after too many injuries with marathons and triathlons, I chose to put the focus on learning to swim with a very competitive adult U.S. Masters team. I was training like a college NCAA athlete according to adults that had been them. Pre-dawn 5:30 am swim workouts, followed by Kettlebell sessions, back to the pool for a double swim session at noon and later hot yoga took its toll.

A brutal punishing schedule and desire to prove myself were familiar. I knew instinctively something was off and I'd have to address it, yet I didn't want to look. The thought of slowing down and backing off did not appeal. It was frightening. I felt I needed that pace to anesthetize overwhelming feelings of being abandoned and valueless and to feel some sense of worth.

After decades of push, push, and then pushing some more, I was finally halted. Running marathons, completing triathlons including Escape from Alcatraz, and working insatiably to become a nationally ranked U.S. Masters swimmer in less than four years ended in my barely being able to make it around my block. I was in excruciating and chronic pain, with simple movements close to unbearable.

Humbled and shocked, I had to let go of another identity. Getting in and out of the car hurt so much that I avoided it. Carefully, I had to think through each step I took to try and figure out which placement would bring the least amount of piercing pain. I didn't want my son or his friends to see my weakened state. I was afraid I'd be put out to pasture, abandoned like a waif if my ambulatory state were revealed for all the public to see.

Still attempting to keep up with my swim schedule I was peppering in some hot yoga to balance it out. I lost almost all rotation in my left hip, necessary to swim competitively. The joint was becoming locked and frozen, my leg shriveling with atrophy. After a year of trying, I surrendered, walking away from all I'd built.

Continuing with hot yoga, I'd pray for a parking space right in front of the studio limping like Frankenstein for the short distance through the front door, down the hallway, and into the classroom, a smile plastered on my face like all was well.

I kept trying to shove myself into positions that no longer suited me. I did not want to let go. It was as if I were a great gladiator who had received mortal wounding, feigning impenetrability. My ego was rupturing. I kept hoping there would be a spectacular solution. Eventually, I had to stop. It was time to look at what I'd run from forever.

Feeling personally punished, I was lost. After so many years of driving my body physically to garner a sense of self-worth and esteem, as well as maintain a fake sense of control, it was time to find another path. I knew it in my heart, though I was stunned and crushed watching another identity fall.

Intuitively, there was no way I'd go the traditional Western medical route of taking out a hip joint that wasn't functioning to my liking to insert titanium. I wanted to give what I realized now was a blessed and miraculous body, every chance I'd never slowed down enough to give it up to this point finding a natural recovery.

A multiple-year odyssey followed with a combination of healing and therapies that worked to tear down strength built on misalignment and rebuild an exhausted joint that was bullied for years. Psychically my hip was screaming for recognition, to address all those anguished unmet needs. The left side of my body was representing an unwillingness to move forward competing with the right side of my body like the Hatfield's and McCoy's. It was a reflection of my own state.

Not with perfection and achievement but with kindness, compassion, and self-care, I was led to a new pathway of healing. It was a way to bring peace where peace was missing, within my own flesh. The war with myself needed to soften, deepen, and dissipate. Although visualization and meditation were helpful to soothe my agony, I needed stretching and strengthening to awaken what had become an atrophied and frozen joint. I had many false starts with healing modalities I was hoping would suffice. Finally, I found the proper combination and things started to shift more consistently. It came in the form of a small group of enlightened experts in Northern California who'd been through their own versions of injury and joint rehabs. Through personal experience, they put the focus on building muscle rather than focusing on pathology, which was revelatory. They were helping people all over the world recover, even from surgeries that had proven ineffective. This was one of the ingredients contributing strongly to my rehabilitation, along with deeply surrendering, listening to my body, and treating it with all the love and care I was able to muster.

Week by week, and month after month, the components of my hip began to untwist, like a rope mop, with each string taking the proper position, reawakening after decades of sleep, and beginning to strengthen. I was walking with less agony and more surety. Though slowly, I started to heal. The amplitude of pain was lessening.

It was difficult to trust the process. It had taken decades for me to reach the state I was in so I assumed it could take at least several more years to find my way back to health. It was hard for my friends to see me, someone who was always active and achieving athletically, grind to an abrupt halt and in agony

CHAPTER TWELVE Controlling Fate with Force

after a few simple steps. Some looked askance at my selected route of refraining from a traditional cut-to-fix western medical approach, yet I was determined to persist.

The healing in my hip mirrored the healing in my heart. Blackened by decades of abuse, both ladled upon me and self-inflicted, the hardened nub began to radiate light, and self-soothing began to melt decades of anguish.

Learning the hard way, I no longer needed to measure my value by athletic achievement. Jumping into a frigid pool to swim close to 4000 meters before 7 am when I was tired, cold, and feeling vulnerable to appease some higher power who would deem me worthy followed by throwing Kettlebells and hours of hot yoga maybe wasn't necessary to find inner peace.

In its place, I was slowly led to waking up, listening to the subtle, as well as blaring calls, my body was transmitting. An evolutionary process, one with its own priceless rewards.

The struggle to surrender wasn't fully complete. I continued to visit the hot yoga room often wondering if that was the best path for the point I'd reached or pushing myself too far. Slowly too, that decision was made for me when I had an episode where my retina could have become completely detached. I had to take time out from classes and detox. It gave me a second round of reviewing what really meant health for my body and to begin to wonder if I was strong enough to make and commit to those decisions.

Instead of sweating bullets in a hot room, I was doing ten-minute ab routines, seven minutes of Qigong, and physical therapy via live stream classes. I thought I'd balloon up a size or two, but interestingly I found that not to be so. Since I wasn't as violently active, I didn't have the need for extra food, sometimes used as a reward for all the punishment, and my body balanced out. In some regard, I looked and felt better than when I was training like a demon daily.

The compulsive need to find self-worth and value through exercise was beginning to erode – a momentous step forward to self-love, and a way of being that brought self-nurturing to the forefront.

I was becoming less rigid in other areas too. I realized I was tackling work projects with much less aggression and letting the timing of the day unveil itself naturally. The fight-and-flight actions of compulsive cleaning lessened. I felt safe to be amongst a dirty dog-haired floor for a moment, not feeling I'd be blown to smithereens.

Oh, and that divorce debt… I whittled it down to the last $3,000 after four years, and that amount was magically gone just a few months later. I was truly out and free. It was a foreign feeling. I was on a path to a more authentic and gentle me.

TOXIC FAMILY

CHAPTER 13
FINDING SOLID GROUND

Respecting my power, loving my own heart, and radiating that to others have become natural. Reclaiming my past and healing my present is helping me to accept my own power stripped away very early on in my journey. Physically, I can't change my childhood. Energetically, I'm continuously learning to recover some of the lost joy. I'm seeing how I've met the difficulty by transforming it from a place of love repeatedly.

A noticeable shift has come in finding genuine compassion for myself. Having had no clue what that meant, it's been key to opening a whole new way of being. Running like an automated, over-achieving robot for so long, my central nervous system was twisted, breathless, and tight. I needed air and light to find rejuvenation and a healthier, less toxic beat. Slowing down, finding my breath, going into my chest and solar plexus, and listening to my still, small, buried voice of soul-based intuition somewhere near my heart has revealed a long-dormant secret. Giving myself respect, and a voice, while taking time to explore how I feel and what I need is changing the way I experience life. It's been easy for me to accept blame that is not mine, trust I'm deserving of hardship, and create it.

Several mentors who taught me about self-love and worth coming from within, rather than without, also led me to discover all I had been through was not shameful but part of a pathway and process to liberation, and a reason I chose to incarnate here on Earth.

Maybe the most radical concept, all those playing their part in my journey are not to blame, carrying out predetermined roles to a T. Because of their courage to play some nasty characters, I'm able to meet all I've come here to learn from and transform. This ideology is big. Letting go of victimhood and resentment to begin to trust myself, as well as others, while forgiving, even the unforgivable, seemed a stretch. Though imperfect, the more I practice forgiveness and appreciation, the more free-feeling and safe I notice I am feeling.

Opening to self-love isn't easy for me. I've never been comfortable looking in the mirror and giving myself accolades as recommended decades ago. I've been able to put into play practical exercises like Matt Kahn's suggestion of putting my hand on my heart and saying, "I love you," repeatedly. Awkward and uncomfortable at first, over time this simple exercise began melting some of the biggest chunks of encrusted rage around my own heart birthing a new form of self-compassion and authentic empathy. My life is getting better.

The "I love you" exercise stretched into further practice when driving my car. Silently I'd begin wishing passing drivers, passengers, and pedestrians what I wanted for myself: peace, abundance, compassion, goodness, light, safety, and joy. I'd recognize I was in fear and projecting negatively on a Monday morning while driving my son to school. Switching the button and spreading positive light with this practice would soon take a chunk out of all those looming fears I was projecting, melting away eons of uneasiness.

In time, this practice began having a profound effect on my central nervous system. Noticing the inner whirlwind of running and achieving like a hamster on a wheel while feeling less-than is being soothed into a more tranquil and loving state of being. A stronger inner voice of compassion is developing and becoming more consistent, recognizable, and steadily leading me to heal.

Being less reactive and coming from a place of greater understanding for myself as well as others is helping me nurture a much wider berth for compassion rather than reaction. While going through this metamorphosis, I did choose to shelter myself, refraining from much social activity, appreciating the quiet of my surroundings, and acclimating to a new life.

Through this period, I've learned I am more of an introvert than an extrovert, something I did not recognize. I could always drum up conversation, approach strangers at a party, and make introductions if I kept my stay short. Afterward, I needed time alone to decompress, find my balance, and connect with my inner knowing.

Shelter-in-place orders during the Covid-19 pandemic helped reflect my love of downtime, yet also revealed I needed a connection with others. This period gave me time to understand what was important to me and ponder how I wanted my own future to look. Another gift of time to reflect was realizing I had new tools in my belt when fear reared its ugly head; to greet and soothe it. I became more trusting in the natural flow. I knew all I would need was available to me or would come my way. This new trust and knowledge allowed me to become more generous. I started giving to random strangers, those who seemed in need and begging on the street corners, from a place of inner joy.

Importantly, I also noticed I was learning how to spot a predator. Slowing my reactions and responses until I was comfortable and grounded to

CHAPTER THIRTEEN   Finding Solid Ground

reply and testing the waters gingerly rather than plunging in offering all have been valuable. Experiences are becoming less about "me" against or completely for "them" and more about breathing and taking space to see a new view of my humanity and that of others with respect and kindness.

My boat can still be rocked. Having deeply profound and excruciating experiences of living this life woke me up to know I am being divinely led by the Universe. All is well and will be well, regardless of outside appearances. I now am understanding this belief to the core of my being. Newfound insight has been worth the price of entry to a place of authentic self-love, self-respect, and well-being, untethered to achievements.

I was unsure I would ever be a parent. My anguished childhood left me wondering if parenting was something for me to explore if I was capable and if that was truly my desire. At forty-two I became pregnant with my son. Honestly, I assumed I was too old to have a child. Most of my younger friends were already trying fertility methods in their thirties. I knew getting pregnant could happen, but thought the odds leaned in my favor of possibly not getting pregnant. When the dipstick turned blue, let's just say I was not rejoicing. It was more of a fearful shock than a celebration. I gained sixteen pounds, terrified my weight would balloon out of control and I'd never recover. I kept to my exercise schedule. Though I did not treasure the physicality of being pregnant, I did connect with the precious being I was carrying with love. Labor and the natural birth process were ten hours door to door.

I remember waiting for the time to push while in the delivery room. My husband was snoring on the cot beside me. I was looking out over the twinkling lights of Los Angeles talking with the soul that was soon to be my son on Earth. I was wishing him well for his journey and assuring him I would do the best I could to help him feel welcome, safe, loved, and whole. I prayed I was up for this incredible role.

I've done everything possible to treat my son with dignity and respect, understanding he is his own being, an individual with thoughts, feelings, and a distinct plan for his time in this world. Giving him the most solid and stable platform I could, and the depth and breadth to be his own being is providing me the high privilege to witness his life unfold. Mothering him and watching him grow has made all I experienced in my own childhood worth it. Like an unexpected gift, the neglect, abandonment, and abuse I survived have given me a clear understanding of what I hope for him and compassion for humanity. It's my hope I am continuing to allow his precious soul to soar while giving myself permission to thrive too. I did my best to break the cycle of abuse and toxicity in the family.

TOXIC FAMILY

EPILOGUE

It's a refreshing place to be once you discover you don't have to fix those you love to feel safe and valued. It's been a revelation to feel genuine compassion toward myself. It's almost like living in a new zip code.

I believe I'm here on Earth to learn through some hard bounces, as well as by joy. It is serving as an awakening. Being pulled through very difficult and painful initiations has led me to a place of more certainty in trusting the natural expansion of my humanity, and a sense of being led by a Divine source.

By acknowledging who I am in truth, a radiant being of light here to spread that light as best I'm able, and come to a greater inner understanding of peace and beauty for us all to take this very moment is a personal mission. Finding delight in knowing my own humanity, honoring my journey, and each day of this incarnation is a profound shift in my consciousness.

I'm choosing to create more beauty, peace, and serenity on this planet for myself and for others. I want to fully embody the phrase: I am the light, the light I am. It's been crucial to forgive, and release the spewing hatred, anger, and destruction within me into a river of violet fire cleansing and purifying my wounds. As I'm coming more from a softening heart, I'm finding gentle strength.

Every bit of the drama and fear I've lived through here on Earth has been a set-up for my soul to evolve. By taking the hand of my wounded child, and embracing her innocence, I am learning to reclaim energy and power otherwise dormant within me. I am choosing to consciously believe and embrace this concept. I believe coming here for human existence is courageous and this journey is an essential turning point for the evolution of my soul. I've been humbled to share my experience with you.

TOXIC FAMILY

A NOTE FROM THE AUTHOR

Life looks and feels differently as I'm willing to implement tools and shift my perspective.

Transformative tools often bring balance, well-being, a sense of peace, and safety into my day.

I'm grateful to be open to teachers of all types who have shared practical wisdom and exercises to help me to evolve. I invite you to explore the following workbook with the hope it will help you in a practical way to find cumulative healing.

Each exercise matches a corresponding chapter from this book.

Often, I've plunged into workbooks with a desire to execute each exercise to some nebulous and unending point of perfection in exchange for assured peace. What I found is there's no special formula to ensure my success, it's an explorative journey.

Take what you like and leave the rest. Start in the middle of the workbook, in the end, or at the beginning. Enjoy each exercise as an opportunity to indulge and explore. My hope is that it leads to the relief of living in heaven here on Earth.

Susan Gold

CHAPTER FOURTEEN Trusting Compassion, Learning to Honor My Humanity

APPENDIX
PRACTICAL TOOLS FOR TRANSFORMATION WORKBOOK

EXERCISE ONE
Understanding the Journey

EXERCISE TWO
Shifting the Underlying Meaning: Seeing Life Experience with New Perspective

EXERCISE THREE
Intuition: Recognizing and Trusting an Internal Gauge

EXERCISE FOUR
Breathing to Find Safety

EXERCISE FIVE
Sound as Healing: Vibration and Frequency Focus

EXERCISE SIX
Self-Love, An Experiential Exercise

EXERCISES SEVEN AND EIGHT
Celebrating Yourself Through Gratitude

EXERCISE NINE
Transformation, Getting to Know Your Emotions

EXERCISE TEN
Finding Greater Power: What's Bigger Than What I've Got

EXERCISE ELEVEN
Your 'Self' in Relationships, Opening to Truth

EXERCISE TWELVE
Connecting Within: Breathing Into an Inner Child

EXERCISE THIRTEEN
Discovering Freedom: Soothing My Inner Terrorist to Find Well-Being

EXERCISE FOURTEEN
Melting Emotions

TOXIC FAMILY

EXERCISE ONE
UNDERSTANDING THE JOURNEY

In Chapter 1, I explore why I'm on Earth suggesting I mapped it all out before entry, looking at my life as if it were scenes from a pre-produced movie, everyone playing their roles with meticulous precision. Looking at one's life in this way, the question "What is this teaching me?" becomes helpful.

The idea of life lessons as a benefit for my soul's evolution is pivotal for me to escape enslaved thinking and to develop a fresh perspective. While uncomfortable, this has led to unparalleled freedom.

In the exercise that follows, be willing to let go of judgments. Halt self-imposed rules as they relate to your responses. It doesn't matter how long or short your answers may be. Allow your heart to speak.

Access the voice within your own heart to halt, become still, and take notice of your breath. Place a hand on your heart toward the center of your chest. Rest your focus at this sacred point and allow your body to gently guide your mind to relax.

You're now ready to write the answers to a few questions...

QUESTION 1. Explore your thoughts and beliefs about why you may be here on Earth. Feel into your purpose and path. Write what comes to mind, even if it doesn't make sense. If insecurity comes up about not knowing an answer, imagine a shower in self-love and kindness and let your pen go free. Allow any feeling of insecurity to filter through your body and pass. Continue to write until you feel complete

QUESTION 2. Describe a specific life experience that has contributed to your current beliefs. It may be a moment of déjà vu or serendipity. Perhaps it is an experience from a dream. Or maybe it's a memory from childhood. Be open to exploration as you describe a life experience that led you to this current belief.

As an example, one of my life experiences was losing my wallet and realizing I may have thrown it out with the trash, which led down a chute, and into the basement incinerator of my apartment building. With help from the building manager, we went down into the basement furnace, poked through the ash and found my wallet, barely singed from the embers, with cash, credit cards, and ID unscathed.

QUESTION 3. Now that you are here, in human form, living on Earth, and experiencing your journey, what would you say to your soul in heaven before you chose this incarnation?

    The first exercise is complete. Take a breath and feel a renewed sense of compassion soaking into your cells.

EXERCISE TWO
SHIFTING THE UNDERLYING MEANING: SEEING LIFE EXPERIENCE WITH NEW PERSPECTIVE

In Chapter 2, I share the experience of my treasured pink baby blanket being burnt by my grandfather with my mom's support. Looking back now as an adult, I see the experience with a broader perspective.

My inner child or soul self was taking on the old patriarchal and matriarchal energy of outdated human thinking and feeling responses. This was a brutal spiritual initiation to learn to see myself not as a victim but to stand above an old, outdated paradigm of male, and female energy, by trusting myself, and owning my power.

Painful initiations often bear fruit to present me with a gift of soul evolution when I have the courage to look deeply with a brave heart. Though not easy, this wisdom has been passed on to me by gifted spiritual teachers.

What follows is a journaling exercise to help you discover your own gift of personal soul evolution.

QUESTION 1: Please write about an experience from your childhood that had an impact, memorable for its trauma, confusion, or pain. It could involve a parent, sibling, or friend. Allow it to spill out of you.

QUESTION 2: Write freely about the pain, injustice, or anger you hold regarding the experience.

QUESTION 3: Now, look at what you've written from a new perspective.
Is there a gift in the experience for you?
What did you learn that is positive?
What has shifted because of your experience?
Describe how this incident served you.

Honor yourself for all you've lived through and for the gifts spiritual initiations deliver.

EXERCISE THREE
INTUITION: RECOGNIZING AND TRUSTING AN INTERNAL GAUGE

In Chapter 3, I talk about intuition. When I was less consciously aware of being intuitive and didn't have experience being judged for my ability, it was easier to accept and seemed natural. Quickly, I hid my capability rather than risk being singled out and punished which often came when my gift was recognized.

Write about a time you remember your intuition leading you to a simple knowing.

Do you remember shutting down this intuitive ability?

Explain an intuitive sign you received – it could be a bird that signaled a direction to take, a picture falling from a wall to help you locate something missing beneath it, or a door that suddenly wouldn't open keeping you from harm's way.

Realize you've experienced intuition. Allow yourself to be open to seeming coincidences and knowing. Trust it is your intuition guiding you. Notice your breath. See if you hear a small voice inside. What is the message?

Applaud yourself for getting in touch with a human superpower.

EXERCISE FOUR
BREATHING TO FIND SAFETY

In Chapter 4, I share that in much of my childhood trust, safety, and security were missing. I had no idea about the long-term impact this had on my central nervous system or sense of self-esteem.

Slowing down, breathing, and taking in life with calm eluded me. As an adult, endurance training, yoga, and meditation served to help assuage some of the trauma. Becoming aware of my breathing has been essential. The breathing exercise I describe below has helped ease scars, lighting the way to feeling peace. I invite you to try it too.

Sit in a quiet place where you will not be disturbed for a few moments.

Close your eyes.

Experience your body as you relax, feel the weight of your body moving down through the Earth. Let your jaw relax and your chest ease.

Now feel your breath going deeply inward toward your abdomen, feeling your lung tissue expand. Release your breathing, slowly, all the way until no air is left in a long slow exhale.

Repeat this process for three cycles or more.

When you feel complete allow your breath to return to normal and gently say silently or out loud:

Mantra: *I am safe in my body and release all energy that does not serve me.*

EXERCISE FIVE
SOUND AS HEALING: VIBRATION AND FREQUENCY FOCUS

One of the themes of Chapter 5 is having trust and self-care trained out of me and then repeating that pattern myself.

It's taken me a long time to wake up to the truth and depth of my self-hate to find the willingness to gently allow healing of any kind.

Music has helped.

Though initially, it felt hokey, I'd find a piece of music with lyrics about love, listen, and then insert myself as the one singing and the one being sung too. It's a gentle way to experience self-love.

When listening or reading the lyrics, see if you can feel the sweetness coming toward your heart as you are singing to and about yourself.

EXERCISE SIX
SELF-LOVE, AN EXPERIENTIAL EXERCISE

A significant transition from high school to a summer job at the shore and then off to college was the focus of Chapter 6. Though I had fantasized about moving on for years, preparing to leave the home I knew was terrifying.

Think of a time you made a transition in your life – a move to a new town or school, a new job, said yes to a new assignment, or made a decision to marry. All these things take courage and can be life-changing. Ignoring fear, I've often plunged right in, taking little time to look back. And I've rarely acknowledged my willingness and courage to take a chance.

In this exercise, hold your hands in front of you gently and with love. Look at them. See the lines that weave through your palms. Think of all you've survived so far. Place your hands over your heart. Softly thank yourself for your journey, your choices, and all the life-changing transitions you have made, no matter how you've judged them or yourself.

Honor your own bravery for being here on Earth, agreeing to have a human experience, and making each of the transitions you've made up to this point.

Send gratitude to your heart. Marvel in the miracle of your journey!

Know that you're building self-love and esteem, and recovering the kindness toward yourself that may have evaporated long ago. Continue this acknowledgment gently going forward into your future.

EXERCISES SEVEN AND EIGHT
CELEBRATING YOURSELF THROUGH GRATITUDE

Moving from college to my first internship position in New York City was something to celebrate, a triumph told in Chapter 7 and continuing in Chapter 8. It was a focus I'd had since elementary school.

Select an achievement or milestone you've created in your life and celebrate it.

What was a transition you made that was a huge moment?

Acknowledge your bravery, small or large.

Put your hands in a folded prayer position.

Bring them to your heart.

Gently bow to yourself acknowledging your accomplishment by celebrating yourself.

Now, consider every person who somehow contributed to that achievement, positive or negative. Feel the goodness of the connection. Send thanks and gratitude to them too, regardless of the role they played.

EXERCISE NINE
TRANSFORMATION: GETTING TO KNOW YOUR EMOTIONS

Subtly knowing or recognizing emotions can be trained right out of us. Caveats like "keep a stiff upper lip", "never let them see you sweat," and "just do it" can support shutting down our feelings and needs.

In Chapter 9, I described my first experience with therapy and learning how to identify my emotions. Though foreign and frustrating, the experience began to melt the hardened shell I had built around myself and brought me in touch with my humanity as well as that of others. Here's an exercise that has helped me to access my emotions while softening the inner anxiety that's been with me since childhood.

Sit quietly.

Go within.

Ask yourself: *What am I feeling?*

Sit with this question until you are clear.

Are you feeling restless, content, angry, or at ease? Try to get a tangible sense of what you are feeling at the moment. Happy, sad, mad, and glad are some basic emotions.

Now ask yourself:

What do I need?

Do I need comfort, solitude, company, or a conversation?

This exercise, though simple, is powerful. The ability to reach my emotions and acknowledge them has allowed profound transformation in my life. It's leading me to treat my body with greater care, pausing at the moment before I respond, drawing healthy boundaries, safely feeling one with others, and less alone.

EXERCISE TEN
FINDING GREATER POWER: WHAT'S BIGGER THAN WHAT I'VE GOT

In Chapter 10, I share needing power and a path greater than myself, realizing I'd created plastic exteriors in an attempt to find internal safety.

Meditating, working in programs, and attending workshops and seminars are all part of it. Ultimately, I need to rely on a power greater than my ego to live fully.

Continual surrender is becoming a friend rather than a strange hardship.

Take out a journal, or notepad on your phone or computer and spend a little time with yourself writing about what helps you surrender to life circumstances, finding trust in power outside of yourself for strength and solace.

EXERCISE ELEVEN
YOUR 'SELF' IN RELATIONSHIPS, OPENING TO TRUTH

In Chapter 11, I reveal the devastation of a relationship motivated by a huge fear of abandonment. I wasn't always fully conscious of my patterning and acted out instead of responding. After some difficult life lessons, I am learning that self-love and self-awareness are necessary to operate at full capacity in a relationship, whether in love, family, business, or interpersonal. If you're willing to try it, come answer some questions with me that may reveal some of your personal patternings when it comes to relationships.

Describe your story as it relates to relationships.

What are your patterns, and beliefs?

Do they feel ancient or current?

Are you happy in a relationship or do you prefer independence?

What are some of your true fears when it comes to being in a partnership?

Describe a time you were authentically yourself in relation to another.

Where do you feel you might improve as it relates to honesty and self-care when it comes to relationships?

If boundaries are confusing and difficult, describe a time when you spoke up for yourself and the outcome it created.

What is your ideal when it comes to setting boundaries for yourself?

Wrap your arms around your torso and acknowledge yourself for being honest with this exercise.

EXERCISE TWELVE
CONNECTING WITHIN: BREATHING INTO AN INNER CHILD

In Chapter 12, I talk about unwinding from harsh self-treatment and the experience of learning to access my inner being.

I've heard for decades about the inner child, small self, little Susie, and found it awkward and almost distasteful, as well as indulgent to consider that concept.

Surprisingly, this has been key to discovering self-love… along with learning to treat me gently.

Find a chair. Plant your feet. Close your eyes or leave them open.

Feel your body in the seat. Feel your feet going through the ground. Now feel your torso. Go into your torso. Breathe. Quietly explore inside.

See if you can sense a still small voice, or a little being, the little you, maybe near your heart.

Breathe some more.

If you feel nothing, it's okay. Praise yourself for being willing.

Breathe.

Acknowledge the little being, even if you're not clearly sensing her or him. Send them love telepathically.

Thank them for remaining with you through all you've been through in this journey.

Breathe.

Come back to your chair.

When you think of it, continue to check in with that inner being. If you continue to feel nothing, thank the nothingness and trust this will shift.

Give yourself love for all you've survived.

EXERCISE THIRTEEN
DISCOVERING FREEDOM: SOOTHING MY INNER TERRORIST TO FIND WELL-BEING

In Chapter 13, I talk about unhooking from beliefs that have kept me trapped, viewing all my experiences from a higher perspective and as necessary rites of passage to transformation.

Take some time now to collect some images that feel good to you. Something that evokes majesty, tranquility, joy, relief, or fun. Print them from the internet, cut them out of magazines, or let your drawing skills come out of the closet!

Build a collage or place your pictures in a magical box, which could be as simple as a shoe box, and make a wish to realize these feelings of freedom and well-being in your everyday life.

Experiencing all you have in life and turning tougher experiences upside down to see what they've contributed to your soul's journey is magical for illumination and the evolution of your soul.

Look at your images and let them bathe your being in the wonder of you.

EXERCISE FOURTEEN
MELTING EMOTIONS

In Chapter 14, I talk about identifying my feelings and understanding my needs.

Sometimes it's frustrating to clearly sense what I am feeling and what I need. I want someone else to do it. Or I'm just not interested in making what seems like a forensic investigation.

Sounding is a fun way to release frustration.

Find a place where you can make noise. Open your mouth, make some noise - growl, yelp, bark, whatever feels good, modulating your frequency up and down.

Start to spin, like a little child on the playground. Turn in circles over and over and let a grin come to your face. Lift your arms from your sides, and feel the release of the turn.

Slowly come back to stillness.

Begin to lift your heels up and down in a jiggly way and add in any sound that comes naturally. Allow this to shift into humming. Feel the vibration.

Find stillness. Acknowledge the release you've created.

MY PRACTICAL TRANSFORMATION TOOLS

Bringing simple and practical tools into my day, on the spot, has the capability of shifting my reality in moments.

These are some simple, one-step, on-the-fly, quick tools I use to soothe fear and rage:

- Breathe in faith, blow out fear.
- Say to yourself or out loud, I release any emotions that are not mine or no longer serve me.
- See a murky, dark mist seeping from your heart, exiting through your chest, and creeping back toward heaven where it is transformed back to love.
- Imagine standing beneath a waterfall that looks violet in color and being showered in the soothing soft purple light.
- See yourself as a towering angel outside of your human body and feel the power of knowing this is you.

I'd love to know how these exercises are working for you and any processes you've discovered and have found helpful.

For information on how to work with me, or for upcoming retreats or workshops, or to reach me directly, please visit susangold.us

TOXIC FAMILY

ABOUT THE AUTHOR

With rural roots in central Pennsylvania, Susan Gold was raised in a challenging and chaotic family system, the middle child of five. Her dream was to exit for New York City or the sunny skies of LA, which both did manifest. To fully thrive, she bravely chose to meet the demons of her upbringing that were continuing to repeat. *Toxic Family: Transforming Childhood Trauma into Adult Freedom* is that journey.

Leaving her little town behind the morning after high school graduation, Susan rarely ever looked back. While in college as a junior at Ohio University, she created an internship in arts management navigating her way to her dream, NYC. Her experience with performing artists like Bill T. Jones, and Paul Zaloom led her into the world of mainstream entertainment after college, first at the global talent agency, ICM and later FOX. Within the entertainment industry, Susan became known for attaching celebrity talent to projects which led her into producing for television and film and a move to Los Angeles.

Susan convinced modern art legend Andy Warhol to do an on-camera commercial for Pontiac; locked in a talent deal for American TV personality Donny Deutsch, which he still claims as one of his best; helped launch FOX News Channel at the request of Chair, Roger Ailes; and on behalf of Disney Channel, persuaded A-list celebrities including Ben Stiller, Jack Black, Taylor Swift, David Beckham and more to be interviewed by the cartoon characters, Phineas & Ferb.

In addition to Susan's business background, she is a decorated endurance athlete having competed in three marathons, dozens of triathlons, and has the distinction of finishing third in her age group at the treacherous Escape from Alcatraz event. Hanging up the grueling demands of her swim, bike, run focus she turned to competing as a Master's swimmer and within four years achieved multiple top ten national rankings including third in the country in the 400 IM.

Susan is a big supporter of helping homeless animals, especially dogs and cats, and helping other business owners move up their career ladder. Her biggest pride is her son, a political science major at the University of the Pacific.

After living with force on both coasts of the United States, Susan heeded an intuitive call for a quieter life connected with nature. She now resides in flow, nurtured by exquisite mountains in the northwest corner of the mystical state of Montana with her beloved partner and their pets. Keen on leaving a legacy to help others heal from similar traumas she's successfully met, *Toxic Family: Transforming Childhood Trauma into Adult Freedom*, her new book is part of that quest. With the same magic Susan created in her career in entertainment, she is now leading retreats, webinars, workshops and private sessions to help others drop outdated storylines and programming in exchange for living from the heart and in authentic freedom as adults.

Published by
TVGUESTPERT PUBLISHING

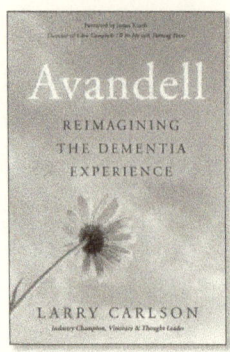

LARRY CARLSON
Avandell: Reimagining the Dementia Experience
Hardcover: $17.95
Kindle: $9.99

SHEILA H. FORMAN, Ph.D
Tame Your Appetite: The Art of Mindful Eating
Paperback: $16.95
Kindle: $9.99

SHEILA H. FORMAN, Ph.D
Mindful Bite, Joyful Life: 365 Days of Mindful Eating
Paperback: $22.95
Kindle: $9.99

MICKI PURCELL
Walking With Anthony: A Mother's Fight For Her Son
Hardcover $22.95
Kindle: $9.99

DARREN CAMPO
Alex Detail's Revolution
Paperback: $9.95
Hardcover: $22.95
Kindle: $9.15

DARREN CAMPO
Alex Detail's Rebellion
Hardcover: $22.95
Kindle: $9.99

DARREN CAMPO
Disappearing Spell: Generationist Files: Book 1
Kindle: $2.99

DARREN CAMPO
Stingers
Paperback: $9.99
Kindle: $9.99

TVGuestpert Publishing
11664 National Blvd, #345
Los Angeles, CA. 90064
310-584-1504
www.TVGPublishing.com

JOANNA DODD MASSEY
Culture Shock: Surviving Five Generations in One Workplace
Paperback: $16.95
Kindle/Nook: $9.99

JACQUIE JORDAN AND SHANNON O'DOWD
*The Ultimate On-Camera Guidebook: Hosts*Experts*Influencers*
Paperback: $16.95
Kindle: $9.99

JACQUIE JORDAN
Heartfelt Marketing: Allowing the Universe to Be Your Business Partner
Paperback: $15.95
Kindle: $9.99
Audible: $9.95

JACQUIE JORDAN
Get on TV! The Insider's Guide to Pitching the Producers and Promoting Yourself
Published by Sourcebooks
Paperback: $14.95
Kindle: $9.99
Nook: $14.95

GAYANI DESILVA, MD
A Psychiatrist's Guide: Helping Parents Reach Their Depressed Tween
Paperback: $16.95
Kindle: $9.99

GAYANI DESILVA, MD
A Psychiatrist's Guide: Stop Teen Addiction Before It Starts
Paperback: $16.95
Kindle: $9.99
Audible: $14.95

JACK H. HARRIS
Father of the Blob: The Making of a Monster Smash and Other Hollywood Tales
Paperback: $16.95
Kindle/Nook: $9.99

New York Times Best Seller
CHRISTY WHITMAN
The Art of Having It All: A Woman's Guide to Unlimited Abundance
Paperback: $16.95
Kindle/Nook: $9.99
Audible Book: $13.99

Published by
TVGUESTPERT PUBLISHING

TVGuestpert Publishing
11664 National Blvd, #345
Los Angeles, CA. 90064
310-584-1504
www.TVGPublishing.com

TARA READE
Left Out: When The Truth Doesn't Fit In
Hardcover: $22.95
Kindle: $9.99

IAN WINER
Ubiquitous Relativity: My Truth is Not the Truth
Paperback: $16.95
Kindle: $9.99

TOXIC FAMILY

TOXIC FAMILY

www.ingramcontent.com/pod-product-compliance
Lightning Source LLC
Chambersburg PA
CBHW031601110426
42742CB00036B/642